The Book on Networks

Everything you need to know about the Internet, Online Security and Cloud Computing

By Robin Fisher

Contents

Foreword

As a coach I am committed to helping people achieve their goals not only in their work life but also in their personal lives. So now, I ask you, dear reader, how do you want the rest of your life to be? Do you want the years ahead of you to be the best years of your life? To do this you need to start by being well-informed, and then take action.

You can achieve more success and happiness in your life if you fulfil your latent potential. To take your business or career to the next level you need to exploit the new possibilities afforded by the internet, the web and cloud computing. If you don't understand these terms or their potential, then this is a must read book for you. *The Book on Networks* by Mr. Robin Fisher will help you understand how our modern connected world works. Almost all fields of business and human endeavour are becoming increasingly reliant on technology and specifically the internet. To be truly successful in any area of life that has any dependency on technology you need to have some understanding of how things work.

By reading this book you will understand how the backbone of our global economy works and with this knowledge comes the prospect for you to take first mover advantage of the opportunities these afford. This book will not only help you to understand networks but will also challenge your existing beliefs of how our connected world truly works. In this book:

- You will understand the history of how our modern connected world came to be. Understanding the past gives you context and helps you to understand the direction the future will take.
- You will understand the technologies that underpin our modern connected world and thus the possibilities that these technologies afford you.
- You will understand the difference between the internet, the web and the cloud, a distinction that will put you ahead of your competition.
- You will learn about the key figures in the history of Information Technology and networking, some of them becoming billionaires in the process and others having a far more tragic story to tell.

Whether you are new to the field of Information Technology or are an industry professional, this book will give you an insight into and a better understanding of the realities of this billion dollar industry.

I know first-hand as a successful businessman that in order to sustain and grow a business you need the right systems in place, systems which today depend on technology. This book will help you understand how these systems work and give you a better idea of how you can leverage technology to help you and your business. One of the key lessons in life that I have found to be true is that if you wish to maintain your level of success you need to keep adapting to our changing world and to do this you need the right knowledge. If you fail to educate yourself, you are setting yourself up for failure. Reading this book will give you the knowledge you need to set yourself up for massive success.

Raymond Aaron, NY Times Best Selling Author

Introduction

Hello, and welcome to the world of networks. These past few decades have seen dramatic changes in the developed world and in how we lead our lives both personally and professionally thanks to the influence of networks and, primarily the biggest network of them all, the internet.

For the last 60 years, computer networking has moulded human history. In the last decade, computer networking technologies have found themselves in the center of worldwide economic crashes, social unrest and revolution, and new forms of authoritarianism marked by increasingly dystopian surveillance states. In this context, understanding networking becomes the tool by which we understand our identities and our societies. It is our mirror, and it is our window into the future we can proactively create. Yet, while networking tools are increasingly user friendly, the history of networking remains dangerously inaccessible to the same people who depend on them for their economic, social and political futures.

Our modern connected world depends on fast and efficient networks to operate. Without global data networks, society would come to a halt. There would be no banking, no Facebook, no email, no text messages and even no phone calls as modern phone systems now rely on data networks to route their calls.

The pace of change continues to accelerate and if you don't understand the fundamentals behind these changes you can easily be left either behind or miss out on the new opportunities these changes afford.

So what is a network? How does it work? What is the difference between the internet and the World Wide Web? How did it all get started and at what personal cost do these new technologies come? Answers to all these questions and more can be found in these next few pages. Should you wish to connect with me personally I can be reached via the website www.thebookonnetworks.com where you will also find additional content available to download free of charge.

Thank you and good reading.

Chapter 1
The History of Networking

A computer network can be understood as a means of connecting two or more autonomous devices via some standard protocol so they can share resources and information in a productive way. The connectivity can be achieved through any wired medium like a normal LAN Ethernet cable, an Optical Fibre Channel (OFC) or via a wireless standard like Wi-Fi, Bluetooth, Microwave, Communication Satellite (SATCOM) and many more. Network software functions on protocols, which are developed and regulated by communities and organizations such as the **ITU Telecommunication Standardization Sector** (**ITU-T**), **Institute of Electrical & Electronics Engineering** (IEEE), **International Organization of Standards** (ISO) and **Internet Architecture Board** (IAB). These and other such standards organisations are usually independent of any one country, and have different countries and companies as part of their membership. Without a set of global standards for communication the world's biggest network, the internet, would not exist as we know it today.

Why do we need computer networks?

A network is required to share data and resources

irrespective of the location of the two connected devices. A basic example is having a networked printer in a home or small office. However, sharing information is far more productive activity than sharing any hardware resource such as a printer or a tape drive.

The modern developed world now has a vital dependence on 'Information Technology'. If a bank were to lose its network connectivity it would not be able to function or even let people withdraw money as it would not know if they had any money to withdraw – such information is held centrally and not locally. Most companies keep customer databases, financial details, inventories, user bases and the like in a centralized location referred to as a datacentre. For any modern company that has more than a few employees or more than one location, a network provides the backbone to the business without which it is unlikely to be able to compete in today's marketplace.

The History of Networks

1955 - 1970: Computer Networking As a Weapon of War

The birth of computer networking and its infrastructure is inseparable from the politics that provoked it. The US government[1], imagining networking as a weapon of war, founded the organization responsible for inventing ways to network computers. It intended to use a computer network to sustain communications and data transfers, even amid potential disruptions of phone and telegraph lines in the event of nuclear warfare.

The Cold War Context

In 1957, the Cold War turned technological when the

USSR successfully launched the Earth's first artificial satellite[2]. Sputnik orbited the earth[3] once every 96 minutes, and communicated via radio signals. The innovation was similar in many ways to Columbus reaching the new world; it set off the race to colonize information gathering technologies.

In 1958, the United States responded by founding[4] the Advanced Research Projects Agency (ARPA), the organization that sponsored research on computer networking, responsible for launching the beginnings of the internet as we know it today.

During this era, research on interconnecting computers was focused on establishing the physical capabilities to allow communication between computers and defining a common language by which two distinct computers could successfully communicate with each other in a potential computer network.

Building the Roads and Establishing the Traffic Laws for Communication

In 1955, before Sputnik was launched, undergraduate student Larry Curtis succeeded in making the first[5] fibre optic cable, strands of intertwined glass as thin as a human hair, for medicinal purposes. Later, telecommunications companies developed fibre optic cables as the highways of the modern internet, used for their capacity[6] to carry digital information over long distances through pulses of light.

While fibre optic cables would take another 20 years to reach the computer networking world, in 1958, AT&T invented the first modem[7]: a device capable of sending signals back and forth between computers through a telephone line. Communication via satellites also became a reality in the early 60s, when Telstar Communications sent television signals[8] across the Atlantic Ocean.

In 1961, only 9,300[9] computers existed worldwide, all used by big companies or academic institutions. One mother computer would be accessed by several different users, using mini computers. These shared the operational capacities of the mother computer via a system called "timesharing." (Timesharing became popular in 1964 with IBM's OS/360[10], its first mass-produced computer operating system.)

Timesharing presented new challenges for data transfer in the world of technologies. Before the 60s, data traveled by way of circuit switching[11]. Circuit switching technology allowed two devices to receive and send messages through a pre-reserved dedicated channel that is best thought of as a road. This road had to remain exclusively available to the two devices for the duration of the data transfer.

While circuit switching is ideal for phone calls that need continuous connections, it is not ideal for data transfer through computers. Computer users are likely to send information in bursts, and reserving an entire "road" means that it might remain unused for long periods of time while clogging up potential traffic from other computers.

In 1965, two computers at the MIT Lincoln Lab were the first to communicate[12] with each other using packet switching[13] technologies, a set of new 'traffic laws.' This technology bundled information into different packets that traveled independently along the 'roads' of the network to later reunite and reassemble at their destination. No reserved road was necessary, allowing computer networks to operate faster and more efficiently.

At the same time as packet switching technology was introduced, IBM developed ASCII[14], the American Standard

Code for Information Exchange, which was the first universal standard 'language' that allowed different computers from different manufacturers to exchange data.

The First Networks Come Together

All of these technologies worked independently, until ARPA became the first agency to successfully use all of them to form a computer network. The first Wide Area Network (WAN)[15] -- a network linking devices over metropolitan, regional and national lines -- came together when researchers connected a computer in Massachusetts to a computer in California using a low speed dial-up telephone line. By 1969, ARPA connected the first four nodes of the ARPANET[16] (the University of California Los Angeles, Stanford, the University of California Santa Barbara, and the University of Utah) using packet switching technology called Interface Message Processors (IMPS)[17].

This growth gave birth to a new issue. ARPANET protocols did not support communication between different networks. This limitation led the researchers to design a communication protocol with more advanced capabilities. ARPA funded this research.

This US government funded research led to the invention of the TCP/IP protocol. TCP/IP stands for Transmission Control Protocol/Internet Protocol. This newer protocol was designed to support communication over internetworks. TCP/IP is still the backbone protocol of internetwork communications to this day.

More networks kept being added to ARPANET so scalability became the new challenge. The distributed naming system of Domain Name System (DNS) was introduced. It provided a mean to associate the numerical IP addresses of computers, resources or services to easy memorable, human-friendly and understandable host/domain names. If, for example, you want to use the Google search engine, you go to the easy to remember google web page (www.google.com or a regional variation such as www.google.co.uk). This is much easier and simpler than having to type in an IP address such as 173.194.41.180.

By 1970, IBM had built online computing[18] into their operating systems. Researchers at ARPA were investigating applications that would allow them to display images on the internet. ARPANET, meanwhile, was using Network Control Protocol[19] (NCP), a set of 'language standards' that allowed different computers to communicate successfully with each other. Academic institutions, operating with the support of the Department of Defense, had used the latest innovations in communications technology to establish a common language and infrastructure that are the backbones for the internet as we know it today.

1971-1990: Internetworks Change Economic Lives

It did not take long for corporations to start using internetworks for their advantages. The dynamic development of private internetworks between 1970s-1990s, in tandem with the growing accessibility of internetworks for both business and personal use, allowed key corporations to use computer networking to dominate local, national, and global economies.

The Early 1970s

In 1965, the year packet switching technology was

implemented, post offices in the United States began using barcodes[20] to scan zip codes. By 1968, the first computers had reached trading floors. By 1969, the first ATM[21] was running in the United States. But it was in February of 1971 that the world's first electronic stock market, the NASDAQ was founded[22], thereby marking the beginning of a new era.

Instantaneous information provided by data transfers through computer networking had become a moneymaker. Later that year, these profit-generating technologies were amplified when ARPANET computer engineer, Ray Tomlinson, invented a file transfer protocol that sent the first email[23] between computers. Two years later, email took up 75% of all ARPANET traffic[24]. Then, in 1972, as CYCLADES[25], the first French Wide Area Network, was established, the first grocery stores starting reading barcodes[26], assigning a number code to each product and manufacturer. Computer networking technologies entered into the personal lives of thousands of people.

1973 saw the development of gateway computers[27], devices that allowed computers to route information between different networks of computers; the first internetworking began in earnest. ARPANET went international, connecting to the University College of London and Royal Radar Establishment in Norway. Finally, the development of the Ethernet[28], a system that connects different computer systems in close proximity using cables, spurred the proliferation of Local Area Networks, LANs[29].

The same technologies that led to the proliferation of internetworks both internationally and locally also allowed stock markets to invade private lives. By 1973, electronic stock markets got a bump when pension funds and endowments[30] started using stock options.

The Mid - Late 1970s and the Construction of the Internet

In the mid 1970s, the internet as we know it came into existence. It began with privatization. In 1974[31], BBN opened a private Internet Service Provider[32], Telenet, the first commercial version of ARPANET, provoking a snowball effect that would eventually shut down ARPANET's successor, NSFNET[33], in favour of an entirely commercialized internet architecture. Meanwhile satellites had established communication across two oceans, linking Hawaii to the UK[34].

By 1976, small satellite dishes[35] made it into residential back yards, and work had begun on a new "language" that could connect diverse computer networks-- from ground based, to satellite, to packet radio. The establishment of the protocol called, TCP/IP[36], marks the beginning of the internet: a decentralized, "open-architecture" system that allows different arbitrarily structured LANS and WANS to interconnect through gateways and routers. TCP/IP would soon become the official protocol for ARPANET[37] and all other networks.

The 1980s and the Virtualization of Our Economy

Online activity among industries exploded during the 1980s. By 1977, AT&T was transmitting signals using fibre optic cables[38] and LANs using the Ethernet[39] were expanding, promising continually faster and more efficient communication technologies.

Importantly, as in the early 80s, Personal Computers became popular and laptop computers[40] were introduced. Telnet software[41], and the later introduction of File Transfer Protocol[42]-- allowing the fast transfer of archives and documents between computers-- added to the functionality that these networks could leverage. In 1982, 5.5 million PCs were sold[43] worldwide. By the early 1980s, companies began to switch from using mother computers, mini computers and timesharing properties, to using individual, desktop work stations[44]. The PC Modem[45] facilitated the change, allowing a growing number of personal computers to connect to the internet.

The needs of the personal computer user, mostly connected using LANS instead of WANS, began to actively shape a burgeoning internet structure. As the first telecommuters began depending entirely on their personal computers to work from home and accessed not only company pages but the first online versions of *Encyclopedia Britannica* and newspapers such as *The New York Times* and *The Wall Street Journal*, the internet was reconfigured to meet their needs. A host of new protocols, including the Interior Gateway Protocol[46] (IGP)-- used to communicate within each region of the internet-- and the Exterior Gateway Protocol[47] (EGP)-- used to tie the regions together-- allowed different networks to use different IGPs according to their individual needs yet still all communicate with each other.

With a more refined internet structure came a more successful virtual economic system. As more companies connected to the internet, the decade heralded the first currency swaps[48], interest rate swaps[49], and stock index options[50]. The growth of a virtual economy based on instant computer networking technologies was aided by the increasing globalization of the internet. By the turn of the century the NSFNET had reached Australia, Germany, Israel, Italy, Japan, Mexico, the Netherlands, New Zealand, Puerto Rico, and the United Kingdom. Meanwhile, the first privately financed trans-Atlantic fibre-optic cable[51] connected New York City with London.

New companies began to form to serve the needs of corporations and individual computer users. Apple[52] and Microsoft[53] became household names in the development of consumer electronics, computer software, and personal computers. The need for computer interconnectivity would soon stretch far beyond the walls of Wall Street and office space. In the next decade, people began to depend on computer networking technologies not only to manage bigger financial decisions such as insurances, mortgages, and retirement plans, but also for the everyday: to order pizza, shop for groceries, and buy tickets to any kind of sports events and concerts.

1990-2005: Computer Networking Restructures the State

In the 80s and early 90s, the geography of the internet expanded dynamically. In 1981, BITENET[54] connected university mainframes worldwide, and led to online knowledge groups and virtual seminars[55]. By 1988, EUnet, the first pan-European Internet Service Provider connected with ARPANET[56]. By the early 90s, Croatia, Hong Kong, Hungary, Poland, Portugal, Singapore, South Africa, Taiwan, and Tunisia had all connected to the NSFNET[57]. The first commercial internet[58] usage was also in full swing.

While the US government first conceptualized the internet as a weapon of war, it had turned into something that increasingly defined the economic and also educational lives of any given state's people. Between 1990-2005, governments reconfigured the way they would interact with the internet, and began using its information gathering powers in ways that redefined the government's control over its peoples' public and private lives.

The Opening of the Internet

During the 90s, not only the economy and academic institutions, but also social groups and individuals began actively using the internet for a variety of networking needs. Their use was facilitated by a number of innovations which quickly made the internet more user friendly and interactive:

In 1991, Tim Berners Lee invented and launched the **World Wide Web**[59], a set of technologies that made it more user friendly to use the internet. The birth of the web drastically increased user accessibility. By 1992, 65 million personal computers[60] were sold world wide, almost 60 million more than a decade earlier. Then, in 1993, the same year that the U.S. White House[61] and the United Nations[62] went on line, the program MOSAIC[63] was released. It was the first software that allowed users to display information graphically on the internet. By 1994, almost one-third[64] of all US households owned a computer.

As computers using a GUI (Graphical User Interface) made the internet much friendlier to use, another tool, the **search engine**, made the internet much easier to navigate. In 1989, Brewster Kahle came out with a publishing system[65] that indexed large amounts of data and made it searchable across large networks. It was a search tool, followed up by Veronica[66], released by University of Nevada in 1992, and Yahoo[67] in 1994.

Meanwhile, intranet technologies[68] allowed the publication of websites and a host of other standardized applications including email, real-time audio and video communication, information publishing, and directories of people, solely for the purpose of inter-company and inter-organizational networking. Intranet technologies allowed the same electronic information to be accessed by any employee on any computer, and unified all the computers, software, and databases in an organization in a single system, allowing for faster, more efficient working environments.

By 1997, there was more email than postal mail[69] in the United States. Internet connectivity only increased as fibre optic cables were constructed, stretching across the Pacific Ocean[70]. Individuals, too, found themselves with options to connect their computers faster and more efficiently to the internet. The Institute of Electrical and Electronic Engineers came up with **WIFI**[71]: a way to connect computers wirelessly to preexisting networks using electromagnetic waves and a wireless router serving as the middle man between the network and the computer.

By the end of the century and the beginning of the next, the internet was entering a new stage.1995 heralded JavaScript[72], an easy to use computer programming language, that is now widely used by websites to make them interactive. By 1998, web publishing tools[73] were made available to non-technical users, spurring the rise of blogs which became popular by the beginning of the next century. By 2001, the year that the interactive and user-based online encyclopedia Wikipedia was developed[74], P2P[75] (peer to peer technology), was on the rise, increasingly allowing networks of two or more PCs that could connect and share resources without the help of a separate server computer. These were cumulative advancements that became known as **Web 2.0**[76]: the technology that brought the internet beyond static web pages, allowing users to interact and collaborate with each other in a virtual community. We look in more detail at the different iterations of the web later in this chapter.

State Interference in Personal Information Aided By Corporate Interests

By 2002, networking completely dominated the private

lives of millions of people. An average UK worker spent more time with e-mail than with her own children[77]. Governments began tapping into this vast virtual world as a means of population control towards achieving their political and economic objectives. For purposes of scope, this chapter will concentrate on the actions of the US government.

In 1995, the Secret Service and Drug Enforcement Agency of the US government first officially used an internet wiretap[78] in their operations. By 1999, in what is considered the first cyberwar, the US government was actively using technology in their involvement with Serbia and Kosovo, to "electronically isolate[79]" then Yugoslavian president Slobodan Milosevic.

The US government's theoretical ability to win wars and push economic objectives through controlling information systems increased enormously during the beginning of the 20th century. The National Security Agency (NSA) teamed up with an increasingly privatized internet and telecommunications network-- dominated by AT&T, Comcast, Verizon, and Google -- to ingest the personal information of millions of civilians. By 2000, the NSA's mission for the 21st Century noted that[80]

"The volumes of routing of data make indexing and processing nuggets of intelligence information more difficult. To perform both its offensive and defensive mission, NSA must 'live on the network.'"

By 2001[81], the NSA was spying on US phone calls and emails without warrants. Between 2002 and 2005[82] the NSA made voluntary agreements for data transfer with several of the largest telecommunications companies, giving the government backdoor access to their communications streams. In an era marked by the foundation of PayPal[83], ecommerce[84], and online banking[85], in which internet phones and cellphones with internet capabilities increasingly defined communication, tracking internet data was a priceless commodity. Through metadata alone, governments began tracking: who you talked to, and who you did not; where you went; what organizations you were a part of; where you worked, what you did in your free time; and how and where you spent your money.

State interference in computer networking means that the boundaries of the state is no longer well defined. The differences between public and private, sovereign and foreign, government and corporation have been undeniably fudged to a point of no return. The US government, and the companies that support them, may know more about your life-- no matter where you are in the world-- than you, yourself.

2005-Present: Social Networking Redefines Democratic Participation

But the birth of internetworking is also a story of a fight over the monopolization of information and the invention of a new, decentralized tool that has dramatically redefined democratic participation. Particularly in the last decade, networking has become a way to dynamically re-conceptualize the way that social movements organize and fight their battles.

Redefining Access to Information

This redefinition finds its beginnings in the way that social networking has changed access to the information that defines our lives. In 1967, the Ohio College Library Center[86] became the first online library. In 1970, AP (Associated Press) was the first news agency to send news by computer[87], marking the beginning of an era began during which people could access and choose between variety of different new sources and opinions. In 1971, Michael Hart started Project Gutenberg[88], which electronically publishes copyright free works, including books. By the mid-90s, all major news sources had websites, and Internet Talk Radio[89] and WebTV[90] had become a reality.

With the advent of Web 2.0 and interactive internet use, people began to both add to and dynamically contest official sources of information. Wikipedia came into being, and blogs and other publishing tools began to go viral at the beginning of the 20th century. News websites began to allow internet users to interact with their articles. In 2001, the Creative Commons[91] created an architecture allowing the sharing and reusing of research and educational material. Finally between 2004 and 2006-- as the $100 laptop computer was developed[92]-- the social networks of Facebook[93], YouTube[94], Skype[95], and Twitter[96] began to create alternate virtual realities cataloguing and defining social interactions both in virtual and "real" worlds.

Virtual Networking and Revolutions

While it is beyond the scope of this chapter to adequately analyze the power of such social networking tools, it is worth examining a few, defining events. As government began to use networking in increasingly invasive ways during the turn of the century, so too did people begin using social networking tools to effectively organize against repressive state structures. In 2002, hundreds of websites based in Spain took their content offline[97] in protest of a government censorship law. In 2003, the first flash mobs[98]-- sudden gatherings of large people who communicate electronically-- were successfully organized over the internet.

In 2006, world power structures took their first big hit as WikiLeaks[99] became a platform for credible information that provides an anonymous platform for whistleblowers to publish information of state and corporate abuses. By 2011, the same year that the US government started the construction of a massive data centre[100] to hold their intercepted communications, the successful people's revolution in Egypt was largely due to the ability of organizers to communicate and share information[101] rapidly via different social networking platforms including Twitter, Facebook, and YouTube. And in 2012, Edward Snowden[102] single-handedly challenged the stability of the US government as world Superpower when he started a global controversy upon his revelations of the scope and details of the NSA spying program. Please see chapter 9 for an in-depth exploration of these topics.

The World Wide Web Consortium

The World Wide Web Consortium (or W3C), founded in 1994, is a group of organizations and individuals who strive continuously to develop and facilitate common standards for compatibility, and to facilitate the long-term growth of the World Wide Web.

The Internet

The architecture of the Internet has changed a great deal since those early days and so has internet usage. Recent data from the Internet Systems Consortium puts the number of internet users at close to 3 billion. Initially, applications such as email, remote-logging and file transfer dominated but now the internet is used for services such as real-time media distribution (YouTube), business shop fronts (eBay, Amazon), media streaming (BBC iPlayer, Netflix), social networking (Facebook and Twitter), information (Google and Wikipedia) and pornography.

How to connect to Internet

To connect to the internet you need to use an Internet Service provider (ISP). Companies that historically provided telephony and mobile phone services have become some of the biggest ISP companies in their respective home markets. For a home user, the most common method of connection is to use the analogue phone line. Historically dial up internet was used for which speeds were limited to 56kbps. With the widespread rollout of Asymmetric Digital Subscriber Line (ADSL) technologies, which allow the telephone line to be used for digital transmissions, internet access speeds for a critical mass of users at speeds of typically up to 24Mbit/s download are now available. Cable and fibre to the home services are also available and can offer bandwidths of up to 1Gig.

Mobile connectivity to the internet

The architecture of mobile phone networks has changed greatly. The first-generation mobile phone systems were based on analogue signals transmitted over the network. Advanced Mobile Phone system (AMPS) was a first generation phone which was widely used in US during 1982.

Second-generation mobile phone systems (2G) switched over to digital transmission for better bandwidth consumption and enhanced security. The voice was converted to digital before transmission. This also enabled text messaging, also known as Short Message Service (SMS). GSM (Global System for Mobile communications), a 2G service, was started in 1991.

The Third-Generation mobile phone network (3G) became popular as it enabled users mobile access to high speed broadband data services. It has become the most successful network in the world with more than 4 billion subscribers worldwide. 3G is loosely defined by the ITU (International Telecommunication Union) as providing rates of at least 2 Mbit/s for stationary users and 384 kbps in any moving vehicle. The first 3G systems were deployed in 2001. UMTS (Universal Mobile Telecommunications System), also known as WCDMA (Wideband Code Division Multiple Access), is the standard 3G system that is being deployed worldwide.

Fourth-Generation mobile phone networks (4G) are now being rolled out internationally but have yet to gain widespread use. 4G provides an ultra-fast internet broadband service typically 5 to 7 times faster than 3G and gives mobile users the sort of speeds they are used to in a fast home ADSL connection.

Web 1.0, 2.0, 3.0 & 4.0

The World Wide Web (WWW) is an overlay on top of the internet. The internet defines the basic underlying infrastructure to allow connectivity. The web can be thought of as how we actually use that infrastructure. As previously mentioned in this chapter, the web was invented by Englishman Sir Tim Berners-Lee in 1989. The first web browser followed in October 1990 and the first web server in November 1990. Sir Tim Berners-Lee's Vision of the web was as follows: "The dream behind the web is of a common information space in which we communicate by sharing information."

What we refer to as the first generation of the web is Web 1.0. This was an early stage of today's World Wide Web seen mostly before 1999. The webpages were usually static and this is now referred to as the 'read only' web. It can be thought of as a traditional library, where you could access but not alter information.

The newer version, Web 2.0, can be described as a generational advancement from static HTML pages to the second generation of World Wide Web that provisions dynamic web with open sharing and collaboration facilities. Web 2.0 presented 'Web as a Platform' on which software and interactive applications would be built rather than the earlier applications which were desktop based only. The common examples of Web 2.0 websites can be today's dominating social media networking sites, blogging sites, video streaming sites, hosted services and folksonomies. This newer version changed the way that developers and end users use the web.

Web 3.0 emerged from Web 2.0 services. It capitalizes on advances in computing to allow systems to analyse information in a human-like manner and then create and distribute relevant content tailored to each individual user. One example of Web 3.0 is a digital video recorder that reviews TV listings and records programs based on your preferences. As of 2014, most services on the web are still from the 2.0 mould and, whilst the progression from Web 1.0 to Web 2.0 took 10 years, it is expected to take a few more years before the move to a Web 3.0 experience becomes commonplace.

Web 4.0 is a hypothetic progression that is still yet to be clearly defined, but the most common expectation is that this is where we would interact with the web just as we would another human, only the web would be more intelligent and better informed than any single human.

Your Life and the Importance of Networking

Computer networks have in a single lifetime gone from being designed as a way for the US military to communicate following a nuclear strike to becoming a dependency for modern life for the majority of people and businesses in the developed world. We may not always realize we are using a network and often take the connectivity and services offered by our networked world for granted. Internet connectivity means access to entertainment resources, social networking, news and the greater sum of all human knowledge.

The history of computer networking technologies is certainly the history of the redefinition of state powers and the undoing of principles of sovereignty that have upheld global political cooperation for the last century. But it is also the history of new and explosive forms to redefine "democracy;" it represents an unequivocal challenge to the information-based power structures that have operated since the advent of published text.

The technologies of computer networking no longer define our lives: they control them.

Today, we are entering an era of pre-crime[103], in which governments use computer networking tools to determine and exterminate potential terrorist targets before they have committed crimes, at unforgivable costs to privacy and innocent human lives. We are also living in an era during which individuals, social groups, and corporations can use social networking tools to their advantages to create their own virtual realities.

Virtual realities are no longer separable from the non-virtual; rather they are intimately intertwined. They no longer simply document "lived" realities, rather they often proactively create circumstances and affect relationships in non-virtual realms. It is in this context that learning to use computer networking tools and understanding the history of networking becomes vital to maintaining sovereignty over our own lives.

Chapter 2

The Protocols used to Provide Connectivity

Network Communications

A good place to start this chapter is with a basic definition of what a network is. Conventionally speaking a network is:

"A set of devices, interconnected via means of communication links."

A device in this sense is also referred to as a node and can be a processing device like a computer or a peripheral device like a printer. The only requirement for it to qualify as a part of a network is its ability to send or receive data to and from the other nodes within the network. It seems like it can get chaotic at times. After all nodes and devices are inanimate objects. They do not have common sense or a little black address book. The internet is an example of a network. In fact it is a composite network which consists of thousands of smaller networks all talking to each other and transmitting data back and forth continuously.

There is one fallacy in our assumption though. If the proper functioning of a network was left to divine intervention, then our world couldn't have quite progressed ahead at the lightning speed it has done over the past three decades. There are an estimated 3 billion computers and other associated devices which are a part of the labyrinth called the internet. But surprisingly enough, most of the time, we access what we intend to and rarely do e-mails meant for one person end up sitting in the inbox of another. The secret is a set of rules governing the communication of the various nodes within a network referred to as network protocols.

A network is basically comprised of two parts.

1. The Hardware which encompasses the devices.
2. The Software which deals with the instructions needed to achieve the desired result from the network in question.

A typical data communication between two nodes, either within the same network or in different networks at two distant corners of the world proceeds in much the same manner. There is a sender and there is a receiver. The sender sends out data, which can very well be text, images or even video and it is received by the correct destination node, almost like the traditional postal service. But in that set up there was a postman who was a human being, endowed with conscious thought and logical decision making abilities. He or she could read the address and deliver the letters and packages to the correct destination. In the virtual scenario there is no postman. He or she is replaced by the network protocol. In order to understand the real workings of how this communication works, we need to look at the layered model of a network. This layered network model breaks down the data transmission between nodes into smaller stages, and each stage is conveniently controlled and mastered by a different set of rules or protocols.

The OSI Model: Open Systems Interconnection Model

The OSI model was the dominant data communications model before the 1990s. It came into being sometime in the 70s and it is an excellent way to understand the structure of the world of IP addresses and data communication.

This model was termed as the "open" model because it was flexible. It allows for hassle free data transfer and communication between two nodes present in two networks with completely different underlying structure. The key is uniformity. The data from a Mac can reach a Windows machine even though the operating system is completely different. Similarly, messages from an office network connected via a wireless network reach a network connected via traditional coaxial cables without any impact on service. The data from different networks is treated the same way and packaged with the same family of headers and bits to provide them with a form which the network interconnection devices (like routers) can recognize and thus send them on their correct path to the correct destination.

The OSI model has 7 layers. The bottom two layers-namely the physical layer and the data link layer deal with the generation of the signals which will constitute the data, the co-ordination of the physical medium required for the transportation of the stream of bits (which make up the data in the first place) and transformation of the raw unreliable transmission facility of the physical layer into a reliable medium.

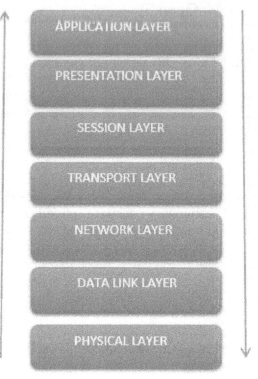

Diagram: The OSI (Open Systems Interconnection) 7 layer Model

Thus the first two layers are chiefly concerned with defining the physical or the hardware aspects of the node and the network.

The next 2 layers up are the Network layer and the Transport layer. Data integrity is of paramount importance when sending data and at the Transport layer there are error detection measures like the Cyclic Redundancy Check[104]. A Cyclic Redundancy Check (abbreviation CRC) is used to detect errors in data transmission. Transmitted messages are divided up into predetermined lengths, the remainder number is then appended onto and sent with the message. The device that receives the message recalculates the remainder and compares it to the remainder that was transmitted. If the numbers do not exactly match then a fault is detected and a CRC error is registered.

Before moving forth to plunge into the intricacies of true internetwork communication, we will take a look at the features which allow for the worlds electronic postal system to function smoothly.

MAC Address and IP Addresses

It has been mentioned a few times in the beginning of this chapter about the accuracy of electronic communications. Without a unique identifying parameter, it is impossible for multiple networks to communicate effectively. In fact, your innocent computer has quite a few addresses.

In this chapter we will focus our discussion on logical, physical and port addresses.

1. **Physical MAC address**- This address is used in the data link layer or the second layer of the OSI model. Your computer, if it is connected to a network, will have at least one MAC address. MAC is an acronym and stands for 'Media Access Control'. Everything that connects to a network has a MAC address. Some devices have multiple devices, e.g. if you have a laptop you will likely have a network card which will have its own unique MAC address and also a wireless card which will also have a MAC address. This is considered to be the lowest level address. When data communication takes place within the same network, the message intended for a particular recipient is marked with this physical address and is delivered to the destination node bearing that particular

address. Most devices have a 6 byte physical address for the nodes termed as the MAC address. As an example the MAC address for the wireless card on my laptop is 58-94-6B-6F-BB-6D.

2. **Logical address**- This is where things get more interesting. The physical address is enough if you intend to communicate with only a small group of devices in your own network. But if you are gregarious and wish to indulge in some internetwork dealings, the physical address is not enough. That is when the logical address comes into action. It is the address which is supplied by the third layer of the OSI model- The Network Layer. The logical address is a universal address independent of the underlying network structure. It doesn't matter whether you are using a windows PC, a MAC or an iPad, the logical address is assigned independent of your physical device type. This logical address is more commonly referred to as an IP address, where IP is an acronym that stands for Internet Protocol. It is most commonly a 32 bit (4 bytes) decimal address separated by full stops, known as an IPv4 address. There are also longer IPv6 addresses which we cover in a later chapter. When you wish to send data to a node which is not in your own network, it is the logical address of the recipient node which you need to stamp the data with and it is this address which gets the job done. An example of such an IP address that you may have on your home network when connected to the internet is 192.168.0.2. You can think of these like phone numbers: everyone who has a phone in the world has a unique phone number when looked at internationally, including international dialling

codes. Likewise everyone who is connected to the internet has a unique address, however this address is normally translated into another address/port combination to ensure it is unique. We will look at this Network Address Translation, acronym is called NAT, later in this chapter

3. **Port address**- This is a very high level address. We have seen that in an internetwork communication, the IP address is vital. Without it there would be no unique parameter identifying the recipient and the basis of internetwork communication would fail. But we need to take into account something else. When we sit at a node like a computer, we rarely dedicate ourselves to one job. We are multi-tasking, reading e-mails, downloading songs or using Telnet. If there is just one IP address for a node, how do so many different streams of data end up at the correct applications? Why don't you receive snippets of the song you were downloading in your inbox? Multi-tasking is possible because of the port address. Each data packet in a data stream is not only tagged with the logical address, but also the port address which is supplied by the fourth layer or the Transport layer. The port address thus distinguishes the data meant for one process from the data meant for another process often running simultaneously on the same node. There are well known ports which are designated for a particular process only- like the port number 80 is used primarily for HTTP or web related processes. When you request to view a webpage, only your logical address is needed, the port number is by default 80.

THE COMBINATION OF THE SOURCE AND DESTINATION IP ADDRESS AND YOUR PORT NUMBER IS TERMED AS YOUR SOCKET ADDRESS. THIS SOCKET ADDRESS IS THE BASIS FOR ALL INTER-NETWORK COMMUNICATIONS.

The Network Layer

The third layer of the OSI model is the network layer. The OSI model was important till the 1990s but after that network engineers and governing bodies saw it best to use a structure that merged the sessions, presentation and the application layer into one comprehensive layer and give rise to the TCP/IP model. The TCP/IP model is defined as the **Transmission Control Protocol/Internetworking Protocol.** Whilst the TCP/IP model is the dominant model used by technology manufacturers in designing hardware, the OSI model is used primarily now as theory and as a way of understanding how things operate. It is an excellent way to troubleshoot problems. If you have a connectivity problem you can work your way up the OSI model to find where the issue is. A basic example would be to use the following process in the event of network connectivity troubleshooting:

First check the physical layer, are the devices physically connected? Next check the data link layer, can you see the MAC address? Next up is the network layer, does your device have an IP address and can it ping any neighbouring devices?

The TCP/IP model defines a number of sets of rules (protocol) for the different layers. The Network layer has the IP protocol, the Transport layer is where TCP and UDP operate and the application layer has a number of protocols the most important of which is HTTP, for which we will come to later in this chapter.

From henceforth we will be discussing all protocols in the context of the TCP/IP layered model.

The logical address is termed as the IP address. The prevalent version of the IP address was IPv4 but presently IPv6 is gaining in popularity, primarily due to the near exhaustion of available IPv4 addresses. The IP address is a unique 32 bits address which identifies all the components of network for internetwork communications. There are two ways in which IP addresses are categorized- **the class based addressing system and the classless addressing system**.

An IP address has 32 bits. Thus it stands to reason that these 32 bits can be arranged in 2^{32} unique combinations which stand at a value of 4 billion. Thus there are 4 billion unique addresses available as the address pool of the IPv4 meaning that if no address translation or other such techniques were used and if all addresses were assigned and in use we could have a maximum of 4 billion different devices connected to the internet. This may sound like a lot but this is actually woefully inadequate for our ever growing connectivity needs. This address pool of 4 billion addresses is broken into a number of classes A, B, C, D and E.

ADDRESS TYPE	NORMALLY USED BY
CLASS A	LARGE ORGANIZATIONS
CLASS B	MEDIUM ORGANIZATIONS
CLASS C	SMALL BUSINESSES AND HOME USERS
CLASS D	MULTICASTING[105]
CLASS E	RESERVED

Each class has a fixed number of IP addresses which have to be allocated if that particular class is being used. For example a large corporation will have to be allocated the fixed number of unique addresses that the Class A designation demands even if some of the addresses are never used by the organization. This results in wastage of IP addresses and thus the **Classless** method of addressing has been introduced. In the classless method, a contiguous block of unique IP addresses is reserved for a particular entity but the number of addresses depends upon the need and the size of the entity. This helps restrict the wastage of precious addresses which have for a number of years been getting close to exhaustion.

Another way of conserving IP addresses is by the means of **Network Address Translation (NAT).** NAT needs a network device that can do these network address translations and can handle a translation table. Before we can fully understand NAT it is important to understand the concept of a **Network Address.**

We now know that an organization is given a block of addresses with which it can identify each component of the network it encompasses. However the first address of the address block is not allocated to any node within the office network. It becomes the identity of the network itself; that is, it becomes the logical address of the router responsible for routing data to and from the network. This address is the network address and it defines the organization network to the rest of the internet. When a node from the rest of the internet sends out a package to a node within the organization's network, it marks the package with the address of the network router. It is the network router which is then in charge of delivering the data to the correct node within the network.

NAT or network address translation is an ingenious concept. Keeping an eye on the ever increasing demand of

IP addresses, the Internet authorities hit upon the idea of private addresses. The IPs from 10.0.0.0 to 10.255.255.255.255, 172.16.0.0 to 172.31.255.255 and 192.168.0.0 to 192.168.255.255 are set aside as private addresses. This means that an organization can use as many IP addresses from one of these 3 private address blocks and allocate the IPs to various nodes within their organization. These IPs will obviously in that case be unique to the organization but not to the rest of the internet where any other entity may randomly choose the same set of IPs. In this case, as previously discussed, the organization device (be it a router or a firewall) is connected to the internet NATs via these private addresses behind a globally unique IP address for any connections to/from the internet. This unique IP address is the public IP address of the organization. The company edge device maintains a table, the NAT table. The simplest NAT table consists of a column for the private address of each node, a column for the port number associated with each private address and another column for the destination IP address for that node. Whenever a node within the organization network sends out data, the router notes down both the node private IP, assigns a port number for the connection and notes down the IP of the destination. When the router receives data, all the data packets bear the same address, the address of the router or the unique network address which is the identity of the organization's network. The router manages to route the packages to the correct destination node by consulting the NAT table. It just looks up the private IP address corresponding to the particular port and destination IP in question and sends the package to the concerned recipient.

Subnetting

Subnetting is a good way to manage large networks. The word subnet is short for Sub Network, a smaller network within a larger one. A very large organization may create smaller networks within the original entity. Each small network is termed as a sub-network or a subnet. The organization is still a single body to the rest of the internet which identifies it with the help of the main network addresses. You can compare this to your home physical address. The MAC address is like your house number, the IP address is the street name and the subnet is your town. Subnetting has many advantages, it allows for large networks more efficiently as multiple smaller networks. If you had one large open network you would have a lot of broadcast traffic which would be inefficient. In addition you would have just a few devices doing all your routing, subnetting allows for you to have multiple devices at different layers in your network to handle the routing of traffic. From a security point of view the segmentation that subnetting gives is also an advantage.

IPv6

The future of the internetworking protocol is without doubt IPv6. It is 128 bits, 16 bytes long which means the address pool can expand to 2^{128} unique addresses for an extremely large number of nodes to connect to the internet. With IPv6 more devices can connect to the internet than there are grains of sand on the earth. The IPv6 protocol has better real time audio, data encryption and authentication and video transfer facilities as in comparison to the IPv4. Since the internet is extremely large and wide spread, some sections are using IPv4 while some sections have moved on to the conveniences of the IPv6 addressing protocol. In order to overcome the problem of a potential protocol clash, either **Tunnelling** (wherein the communication between two IPv6 nodes must pass through a region of IPv4 protocol, hence the data packet is encapsulated in an IPv4 packet to help make the pass) or **Header Translation** (wherein an IPv6 node wants to communicate with an IPv4 node and the whole header is translated from the IPv6 protocol to the IPv4 protocol) is used. Thanks to these techniques IPv4 and IPv6 networks can work in parallel. As the majority of IPv4 addresses have been allocated an increasing number of new network connections to the internet will, in the future, use IPv6. An example is mobile connectivity where a number of service providers in different countries have already adopted IPv6.

The Transport Layer

We have previously mentioned that the Transport layer is the fourth layer of the TCP/IP model. It is another vital layer which ensures the correct delivery of traffic in an internetwork. The two most important protocols of the Transport layer are the UDP and TCP protocols.

UDP- UDP is an acronym for the **User Datagram Protocol**. We know that the Transport layer works to send relevant data to the correct port of a particular node which is running simultaneous processes. UDP is a connectionless and thus unreliable method of sending the datagrams to the concerned ports. There is no establishment of a connection between the sender and the receiver and there is minimum overhead involved. We know that the message from the application layer is chopped into data packets or datagrams. These datagrams are thus components of one long message. In UDP however, no sequence number is provided to these Datagrams. They are stamped with only a **16 bit address of the sender's port and 16 bit address of the receiver's port**. They trickle down to the Network layer where the packets are tagged with the IP address of the destination and off they go into the abyss of the internet. The UDP thus imposes no error control and is considered an unreliable protocol. It is good for one to many broadcasts such as multicasts, which we will cover in a later chapter.

TCP- TCP is an acronym for the **Transmission Control**

Protocol. It is the antithesis of the UDP and thus it can be described as a reliable, connection oriented service. With UDP the message is chopped into Datagrams and these datagrams recognize no relationship between each other even though they are part of the same message. But in case of TCP, the delivery of the message as a stream of bits is facilitated. There is an imaginary tube like connection or pathway from the sender to the receiver through which the stream of bits move. Only when the whole message is accurately delivered to the destination is the connection terminated. **In TCP there has to be an acknowledgement from the receiving end for each bit of data or otherwise the sender will resend the data.**

Data Transfer in TCP

The actual data transfer process as part of the TCP is composed of three tasks:

1. **Connection Establishment** which involves a 3 way handshake.
   a. **SYN:** In this the sender sends out a synchronization segment to the receiver so that their speeds of transmission and initial states can be synchronized.
   b. **SYN-ACK:** The receiver replies back with a synchronization plus acknowledgement frame.
   c. **ACK:** This is followed by a final acknowledgement frame from the sender to tell the receiver that both sides are now in perfect understanding and thus data transfer can begin.
2. **Data transfer** between the sender and the receiver
3. **Connection termination** which proceeds via a 4 way handshake to ensure that each side of the connection is terminated independently.
   a. **FIN:** Sent from initiator to receiver

b. **ACK:** Sent from receiver to initiator
c. **FIN:** Sent from receiver to initiator
d. **ACK:** Sent from initiator to receiver

TCP is the best choice for communications which need reliable data transfer.

Application Layer Protocols

We are now more or less versed with the way data transmission takes place between various nodes in networking scenarios. The last layer to be investigated in terms of data transmission is the Application layer. It is responsible for acting as a friendly interface between the lower layers of the model and the human user who may not understand the datagrams and bits of the Network and Transport layers, it is essentially the user interface.

Some common protocols of the Application layer include:

1. **SMTP- Simple Mail Transfer Protocol** is the protocol governing the sending and receiving of e-mails. It defines the commands and responses of the client Message Transfer Agent which is at the client's side and the receiver Message Transfer Agent which is at the server or the receiver side.
2. **FTP- File Transfer Protocol** is responsible for controlling the transfer of files between two systems. It facilitates the hassle free transfer of files even if the two systems have completely different file structures and text representation schemes. In FTP there are two connections established between the systems- one for transmission of the actual data and the other connection is for the transmission of control related information so as to co-ordinate the reception of the files.
3. **HTTP- Hyper Text Transfer Protocol** is what you normally use when you browse the web using a

web browser such as Internet Explorer, Chrome or Firefox. **It is the preferred protocol of the World Wide Web**. Thus when we wish to view a web document on our browser, we are governed by HTTP. The messages exchanged between the client (you) and the Server (the website) are called Requests and Responses respectively. HTTP uses TCP as a connection oriented Network protocol. An HTTP connection is either **persistent** (after one request is satisfied the server keeps the TCP connection open for further requests) or **non-persistent** (after a response has been received from the server, a new TCP connection has to be initiated for further web transactions). There is also a more secure form of HTTP called HTTPS, with the S standing for secure.

Networking is a fascinating subject. We may not be able to actually see any of the processes delineated here with the human eye, but the results are always consistent with the rules. We owe a large part of the recent prosperity of the human race to networking principles and discoveries. This quote by the late visionary Steve Jobs proves the immense potential of networking even when it was in its nascent stage:

"The most compelling reason for most people to buy a computer for the home will be to link it to a nationwide communications network. We're just in the beginning stages of what will be a truly remarkable breakthrough for most people - as remarkable as the telephone."

Chapter 3

Local Area Networks and Physical Connectivity

Cables and Cards: The Foundation of Computer Networking

Websites get all of the attention, but it's network cables and network cards which power the Internet. Together with routers, switches, and other technology, they make possible the incredible feat of watching online video or playing an online game with only a barely-noticeable delay. Computer networking is marvelously simple in abstract but quite sophisticated when you examine the details, and the details all start with the hardest-working and least-appreciated part of computer networking—the cables.

Cables: What They Do Is Obvious; How They Do It Is Not

Most computer networking cables are made of copper wires coated in plastic. They work much like any electrical cable: electrons pulse down the cable at approximately 60% the speed of light. By modulating the pulse, a device at one end of the cord can communicate with a device at the other end of the cord.

The most common networking cable in home and small office use is a CAT-5 or CAT-5e Ethernet cable. The CAT (which is often uppercased) stands for Category, and the number and optional letter following it stands for which category. Ethernet means the cable is designed to transmit Ethernet signals; but Ethernet signals can also be transmitted using other types of cable.

One of the reasons CAT cables are widely used is their innovative design which reduces costs. Unlike other cables which preceded them, CAT cables use pairs of tiny wires to eliminate most electrical interference (crosstalk) from nearby cables. Cruder types of cables, such as coaxial, require shielding to be installed above the cable, which adds significantly to costs.

In any electrical cable, eliminating crosstalk is essential—crosstalk causes lost data, and crosstalk tends to increase as electrical activity increases, so the less crosstalk in a cable, the higher bandwidth it can support. For example, CAT-5e is nearly identical to CAT-5, but it eliminates some extra crosstalk, allowing it to support bandwidth up to 10 times higher than CAT-5. CAT-6 further reduces crosstalk and can support bandwidth up to 10 times higher than CAT-5e, or 100 times higher than CAT-5.

Measuring Bandwidth

The more bandwidth a cable supports, the more data it can send in a single second. Bandwidth is typically measured in bits, which is the value of a single virtual switch which can be turned on or off. Programmers represent on and off using binary ones and zeroes, respectively. The digital representation of each letter in this paragraph uses eight bits. (For example, the code for the letter E is 01100101.)

Most computer users think in terms of bytes—particularly megabytes and gigabytes. It takes eight bits to make a byte, so one megabyte equals eight megabits.

CAT-3 (no longer used) supported bandwidth of up to 10 Megabits Per Second (Mbit/s), sometimes called 10BaseT; that's means you can download (at max) a little bit over 1 megabyte each second. CAT-5 (there is no CAT-4) supports bandwidth of up to 100 Mbit/s, sometimes called 100BaseT or 100BaseTX, which maxes out at a little over 10 megabytes per second. The X in 100BaseTX means CAT-5 can send signals in both directions simultaneously (called duplexing) so you can download at 100 Mbit/s and upload at 100 Mbit/s at the same time.

CAT-5e bumps bandwidth up to 1,000 Mbit/s (1000BaseT or 1000BaseTX) for roughly 100 megabyte per second downloads. CAT-6 can theoretically run at 10,000 Mbit/s, also called 10 Gbit/s, (10GBaseT) to let you download at about 1 gigabyte per second, although CAT-6 equipment is still relatively new and unproven.

Attenuation and the Switch to Fibre Optic

All CAT cables are limited to a maximum length of 100 meters (328 feet) because electricity over copper cables loses its ability to carry data the further it travels, a process called attenuation, and the delicate electrical modulation required by Ethernet over CAT cables cannot survive cables which extended beyond 100 meters.

To deal with attenuation, long-distance computer networking uses fibre optic cables. Because fibre optic cables use light, they don't need to worry about electrical crosstalk, so speeds tend to be much higher.

There are two main types of fibre optic cables, single mode and multi-mode.

- Single mode fibre can be used for distances up to 100km and has bandwidths of up to around

10Gbit/s
- Multi-mode fibre can be used for distances of up to 1km but has bandwidths of up to around 100Gbit/s.

Although Ethernet over CAT cables rules high-speed short-range networking and fibre optic service rules high-speed long-distance networking, there's another set of technologies which rule medium-speed short- and medium-range networking—wireless networking.

Wireless networking uses radio signals and has to deal with many issues wired networking does not, such as the multiple receivers, transmission range, and wireless security. These issues are addressed in Chapter 5 so here we will simply treat wireless networking as a virtual cable between two computers or devices.

Cable Connectors: What Makes Cables Work

A cable can't do very much until you attach its ends. In some cases, a type of cable has only one common end. In other cases, there are lots of different types of cable ends which can fit the same cable.

- Ethernet cables most commonly use RJ-45 connectors. They look like large phone connectors, which isn't too surprising since both Ethernet connectors and phone connectors (RJ-11) use Registered Jack-style (RJ) connectors.
- Fibre optic cables use a number of different connectors—each long-distance fibre optic business can choose what connector they want. In the United States, most home and small business subscribers to fibre optic service have a Subscriber Connect (SC) connector.
- Both copper and fibre optic cables can connect to a Small Form-factor Pluggable (SFP) transceiver—a

clever little device which translates either electrical signals or optical signals into a standard set of electrical signals a computer can interpret.

Of course, on the other end of connectors is the device which transmits and receives signals over the cord.

Transmitting and Receiving Data between Devices

Devices which transmit and receive data are much more complicated than the cords or radio signals which carry that data. Modern high-speed communication equipment faces two competing problems: how to increase bandwidth while simultaneously reducing response time (which is called latency).

Latency is influenced by a variety of factors, the most obvious being cable length. Both copper and fibre optic cables transmit signals at roughly 200,000 kilometres per second, or a bit over 60% of the speed of light in a vacuum. That means that a signal traveling through the underwater fibre optic cables between New York City and London (5,500 kilometres) has a minimum latency of 27.5 milliseconds one-way. Latency is often measured in Round Trip Time (RTT), so the minimum RTT between London and New York City would be 55 milliseconds. When you do a ping on your computer to an address the response times you see are the RTT, so the time it takes your packet to go from your device to the destination address and then respond.

At each end of the fibre optic cable, machines convert the fibre optic light signals into electrical signals and electrical signals into fibre optic light signals so computers can process and route the data. This conversion adds to the latency—the fastest advertised transatlantic fibre optic cable has a minimum RTT of 62 milliseconds—7 milliseconds longer than it takes light to travel that far.

A tool built into Windows, Mac, and Linux makes it easy for anyone to test latency between their computer and a remote Internet server. The tool's name is `ping` and you will need to start a command line (terminal) in your operating system to access it. In the below example the actual RTT latency from Newark, near New York City, to the official Transport for London website server is measured:

```
$ ping tfl.gov.uk

PING tfl.gov.uk (217.28.130.140)
56(84) bytes of data.

64 bytes from 217.28.130.140:
icmp_req=1 ttl=243 time=72.0 ms

--- tfl.gov.uk ping statistics ---

1 packets transmitted, 1 received, 0%
packet loss, time 0ms

rtt min/avg/max/mdev =
72.045/72.045/72.045/0.000 ms
```

It took 72.045 milliseconds (ms) for the "ping" to get from New York to London and back. That's 10 milliseconds or 16% longer than the advertised minimum latency. Where did the extra latency come from? By replacing the ping command with the traceroute command (the actual computer command is spelt tracert) you will be able to see more information such as the actual path the data followed. An examination of the traceroute results above shows that approximately 12 devices besides the test computer and the London computer processed the data on its way back to Newark from London. (There's no way to see how many computers handled it on its way to London without having access to that London computer.)

What were those 12 devices and what did they do in those 10 milliseconds?

Following the Signals

The server which sent the ping from near New York City used a standard 100BaseTX (100 Mbit/s) Ethernet Network Interface Card (NIC) connected to CAT-5 cable.

Modern Ethernet devices all have a Media Access Control (MAC) address which helps them communicate with other Ethernet devices on the same physical network. This is separate from an Internet Protocol (IP) address which helps computers connect to each other across multiple networks (that is, across the Inter-connected Network, or Internet). See Chapter 2 for more information on MAC and IP addresses.

When the server tried to send the ping request through its network card, the network card converted the ping into data that could be understood by other Ethernet network cards. Large chunks of data are split into small pieces because the maximum amount of data Ethernet will transmit at the same time on a 100BaseTX network is 1518 bytes—that's the equivalent of 1518 typed English letters, or roughly equal to 1/10th the length of this chapter in plain text.

After splitting the data into chunks, the network card adds a header and footer containing the MAC address of the sending network card and the MAC address of the intended recipient network card. Adding addresses might seem unnecessary since the sending computer or device is usually connected directly to the receiving computer or device. But earlier in Ethernet's history (and still used rarely today) multiple Ethernet devices could connect to a hub which would broadcast each device's data to all the other connected devices, so each network card had to filter out just the data addressed to it. For this reason, 802.11-

style wireless devices which frequently receive data broadcast by other wireless devices also use MAC addresses.

In Ethernet networking, the header plus data plus footer is called a frame. Once the network card constructs the frame, it transmits it. In this particular frame from the server near New York City, the data contains all of the information necessary to route that data using the Internet to London, and the header and footer include the server's MAC address and the address of the next device on the way to London—the switch.

Following the Data Hop-By-Hop

The server's network card transmits the frame over the CAT-5 cord; that cord leads to a networking switch, named after old-style telephone switchboards run by operators who figured out how to connect one phone with another. A network switch figures out how to connect one computer with another, and by doing so it creates a Local Area Network (LAN) which lets computers communicate with each other using IP addresses in much the same way you and I can communicate using telephone numbers.

The switch's network card receives the Ethernet frame, sees its own MAC address in the recipient field, and extracts the data. If the data is a small part of a larger piece, it waits for other frames to arrive with the remaining pieces and then hands all of the data up to the switch's operating system. In this case, the switch's operating system sees that the data is trying to get to London. Switches have multiple network cards so they can talk to multiple computers or other switches. The switch's operating system consults a table of its different network cards and finds one that connects to another switch which is a little closer to London. It hands the data to that network card and the network card sends a new Ethernet frame to that new switch.

Two bits of reality intrude upon the abstraction described above: one, the switch's operating system probably isn't like Windows or Mac OSX. Modern switch operating systems are implemented entirely in hardware to make them run incredibly fast, keeping latency low and allowing the switch to provide enormous bandwidth. Two, the switch's operating system doesn't know which other switches are physically closer to London, but it does know which other switches have done a good job in the past of getting data to London fast, so it uses them.

In the same manner as described above, the data travels from switch to a router. A switch is generally used as a device to connect multiple devices such as computers to a network. They are generally used in environments such as offices. A router is used primarily, as the name suggests, to route traffic. You can get switches that are also routers but once you get into the core of a network or the backbone of the internet you will find dedicated routers. Routers know where to send traffic as they hold a routing table. This is a table of all the subnets that it knows about and for every subnet it has a next hop address, where to send any data for that subnet to. Any internet router would also participate in the internet routing table and advertise to its neighbours its own and its connected subnets. In this way, any traffic wanting to come to anything connected to this router can now find a way. The internet routing table as of April 2013 was in excess of 450,000 routes.

Going back to the journey of our data we know that a radical transformation occurs somewhere in this trip—at some point the data gets changed from electricity over copper wire to light in fibre optic conduit so that it can travel under the Atlantic Ocean. Yet, the method is fundamentally the same: a copper-based network card in a router receives the Ethernet frame containing the data, it hands the data to its operating system, its operating system determines that the best way to get to London is to use one of its fibre optic-based network cards to connect to another router, so the operating system hands the data to that network card, the network card constructs a frame, and the data is sent to the next router over a fibre optic cable.

In the steps above, we observe the data going from the outer layers of network equipment towards the inner layers. The outer layer is called the access layer because it gives end-user devices access to the network. The middle layer is called the distribution layer—it connects whole sub-networks of devices together, such as businesses or thousands of users on a local Internet Service Provider (ISP). The innermost layer, the core layer, simply moves data in bulk from one place to another. Each layer usually uses different equipment—but sometimes the same piece of equipment performs multiple functions to increase performance. In smaller networks, the same network hardware might be used for both the distribution and the core network; this is called a collapsed core.

Eventually, the data arrives in London. In this case, the data was a tiny little bit of information which requested the London computer send a reply back to the server near New York City. The London computer agreed and all of the previous steps were repeated. It's possible the same path and the same routers were used, but it's also possible different routers and a different transatlantic fibre optic cable were used—each router along the path gets to choose the next router, so data can take a multitude of paths.

But no matter what path gets selected, the network cards and cables you've just learned about will continue to do their simple—but essential—jobs.

Chapter 4

Metropolitan and Wide Area Networks

The constant need for communication has led to a way of connecting computers together, in such a way that they can share information and resources. This is what, today, we call - a network. A computer network is a collection of two or more computers that are interconnected.

The internet is a network of networks, a web across the globe, keeping people in touch, filled with information for and from nearly everybody, the backbone of our modern society that connects billions of people worldwide.

In this chapter, we'll take a detailed look at what networks are, their different types, and how they are used in real life.

Introduction to LAN, MAN and WAN

What happens when networks get bigger than your simple home network? How does their technology differ from what you can buy at the local retail technology store?

There are different kinds of computer networks, and they can be classified in many ways. The most common classification of networks is by their scale or scope. The networking industry refers to these different networks by the area they cover.

Here follows an explanation of these network classes in ascending order of network coverage.

LAN

A local area network or LAN is the smallest and most basic form of networking. The coverage area is quite small.

LANs mostly cover a home or a single building or, at the most, a small group of buildings. They connect a group of personal computers or workstations.

Each computer or device is a node in a LAN and executes its own programs independently. Additionally, each node can also access data from other nodes within its LAN.

For example, consider a LAN where a small group of computers and printers in an office are connected to each other. On this network, users will be able to share and access data located on other computers within the LAN. They will also be able to send print commands to the printers on the network and users will be able to communicate with each other through network applications, e.g. company instant messaging systems such as Microsoft Lync.

The small size of a LAN enables fast data transmission speeds between the nodes. However, the biggest limitation of this kind of network is the distance it can cover. Most LANs are connected with Ethernet cables which have a physical limitation on their length, this is covered in detail in Chapter 3.

One consideration when designing a large LAN is a broadcast domain. A broadcast domain is a network segment where a single broadcast from any device on the segment goes to all other devices on the segment. If you were to have thousands of computers connected in a single broadcast domain the devices would all have to process the broadcasts which may lead to re-transmissions and impact performance. A broadcast domain is broken up by the placement of switches and routers and the configuration of VLANs. Avoiding broadcast storms is one of the reasons why it's important to ensure proper network design when your network grows in size or number. So long as you properly segment your network using subnets and route all your traffic efficiently a properly designed and managed large LAN can be as efficient as a small LAN.

WLAN (Wireless Local Area Network)

The wireless network of computers and mobile devices connected through a wireless router you find at homes and small offices is an example of a small WLAN (Wireless Local Area Network). Quite often, a WLAN is either a separate network or a supplement to a wired LAN.

Computers and devices within the geographic range of a WLAN signal will have the ability to connect to it, providing they have the requisite security credentials. In a home environment an ADSL router provided by your ISP will generally also provide a wireless network. The range of this will depend on signal interference which can come from other electronic devices, but is normally caused by walls and floors, particularly if they are solid in nature. The range of wireless signals can be extended using boosters or deploying multiple wireless access points, an access point being a device that provides a wireless signal and thus wireless connectivity. Whilst a single wireless access point may only have a range of anything from 10 to 30 or more metres depending on the signal strength and the environment, installing multiple access points ensures that you can provide wireless connectivity for a whole building, site or campus network. Different standards associated with WLAN allow for different data transfer speeds ranging from 11 Mbit/s to over 1Gbit/s.

Security is always a consideration with a wireless LAN since anyone within the geographic range of the signal can see the traffic, but modern encryption protocols, if properly implemented, keeps the data secure.

For a detailed look at wireless technologies and wireless LANs (WLAN) please see chapter 5 which covers these topics in detail.

MAN

A metropolitan area network or MAN covers an area larger than what can be covered by even the biggest local area networks. The term MAN refers to the interconnection of various networks within a city to form a single large network. These MAN networks work like an internet service provider or ISP. However, a MAN is sometimes not used by a single organization.

A MAN is also sometimes called a campus network, in which case several local area networks are bridged by backbone lines to form a single network.

MANs have been set up in various metropolitan areas, including London (England), Geneva (Switzerland), and Lodz (Poland). Despite their name, MANs are not restricted to metropolitan areas. They are also used in large universities, and wireless MANs have also become feasible in recent times.

A MAN is very efficient and usually provides rapid communication through fibre optic cables or other high speed connections. It is an ideal choice for those who want a medium-sized network with fast data connections for towns, cities, or large campuses. Computers connected to a MAN usually have access to shared resources and the option to transfer data at high speeds; this includes high quality audio and video.

Some large companies use MANs to connect all their sites within a geographic location together, e.g. all sites in one country or in a few neighbouring countries and then connect this MAN into their global network backbone, usually with 2 separate connections for resilience.

WAN

WAN – Wide area Network, the term basically defines an "extended network". WAN is a network that connects neighbourhoods, cities, sometimes even countries or regions. They often connect several smaller networks, like LANs and MANs. The internet is the biggest and most popular WAN and is itself made up of multiple LANs, MANs and other smaller WANs.

Usually, WAN networks include public lines of communication and the necessary connective elements. They are used to connect LAN and other types of networks in order to facilitate communication, between people and devices separated by great distances.

Some companies and organizations have built their own WAN networks but the majority enlist the services of internet providers, which provide them with WAN connectivity.

Although WANs are similar to Local Area Networks, there are important differences. For starters, they don't connect individual computers, but generally they connect whole LANs together. WAN connections generally have a much reduced bandwidth when compared to LAN and WAN connections. The upside is that they cover a much greater distance. Whilst your LAN is linked to specific geographic location and your MAN is limited to a geographic region, your WAN can connect sites anywhere on the planet.

Whilst most large companies have their own WAN networks we will look in detail at two WAN networks in the United States of America. The first is maintained by the U.S. Department of Defence (DOD), called the Secret Internet Protocol Router Network (SIPRNet) and the second one we shall look at is maintained by a collection of educational institutions, called Internet2.

SIPRNet: A WAN For Private Communication

As its name suggests, the US DOD uses the Secret Internet Protocol Router Network (SIPRNet) WAN to send confidential communication from one site to another. Although many details about SIPRNet are classified, it is widely known that SIPRNet uses leased and government-owned fibre optic cables to connect all major military bases in the U.S. This so called Secret network not proving as secret in reality as the US government would like.

Because the government controls both ends of each fibre optic cable, it can transfer data with much more security than if it transmitted that data over the public Internet.

The government can't guard all of its thousands of miles of buried fibre optic cable, but here WANs give the government another edge over the public Internet. Because the government controls its entire WAN, it can choose what data transfer protocols are used. Although the exact protocols used are classified, we can confidently assume that all data sent over SIPRNet is encrypted.

Internet2: A WAN For High-Speed Communication

The original Internet was designed for the DOD mostly by various universities and, for many years, the DOD and universities were the only significant users of the Internet. But as the Internet became popular with businesses and consumers, the amount of bandwidth available to universities dropped. Universities responded by building their own "Internet", a WAN called Internet2.

Although Internet2 has gone through several iterations, what it offers today is probably the highest-bandwidth long-distance WAN in the world, with lower latency than any long-distance commercial network. The high bandwidth lets supercomputers located across the country work together to solve difficult problems, and the low latency has allowed surgeons to remotely operate on patients in different states.

With commercial Internet providers offering higher bandwidth and lower latency with each new generation of technology, most businesses and other organizations today don't need a WAN for bandwidth or latency reasons. Instead a lot of modern businesses leverage the internet for their WAN networks and secure their traffic by using a technology called a Virtual Private Network or VPN for short, a topic we shall look at in detail later in this chapter.

MPLS

Multiprotocol Label Switching or MPLS is a standardized technology that is often used by ISPs to provide WAN services for medium to large companies. Not only does MPLS allow you to prioritise your traffic but it also speeds up network traffic flow.

It involves setting up and designating a path for packet sequences. Labels are added to each data packet so that the router does not have to look up the address in the full routing table but rather just references the short path label.

Effectively the traffic is routed at layer 2 (switching) rather than layer 3 (routing).

The term multiprotocol refers to the network's use of Internet Protocol, Frame relay network protocol, and asynchronous transport mode (ATM).

MPLS, through label switching, makes network traffic move faster than comparable technologies and can apply quality of service to a network. Historically MPLS was the primary choice for providing a WAN service to medium to large companies, but this technology, when compared to the cost of an internet connection, is expensive. Increasingly large companies are leveraging cheaper internet connections and securing their data with a VPN to give them nearly the same level of service but at a much reduced price.

VPNs (Virtual Private Networks)

Our dependence on internet connectivity for consumers and organisations continues to grow each year and with this growth comes the need for privacy. We now use the internet for, amongst other activities, shopping, for fun, to meet people and to work. We send out information about us, about our families, our work, our bank accounts and we most certainly want that information to remain private.

We also need a fast and reliable way to communicate and share data securely over networks that we do not own or control, such as the internet. This can be achieved using a VPN – a Virtual Private Network.

A Virtual Private Network is a virtual tunnel (or a bridge) that provides a direct point to point connection to a private network, through a shared or a public web, such as the internet. All the data that you transfer is encrypted, therefore you don't have to worry about exposing private information over the internet. The basic technology used by a VPN is cryptography. At a basic level cryptography lets two computers agree on a cipher—a secret code—and then send messages using that cipher which no other computer can read. You use cryptography whenever your computer connects to a website whose address starts with "https"—the S stands for secure, and the security used is a form of cryptography. See Chapter 7 for a more in depth look at network security.

A Virtual network means that it doesn't exist physically; it is built over an already existing network. The VPN is normally configured with encryption to provide a level of assurance that all the information you send out and receive through this "tunnel" remains confidential.

There are no set standards on how VPNs are set up. Companies planning on setting up their own VPN should decide the components and protocols to use according to their means and requirements. The more encryption you use the higher the overhead for your devices, so choosing the most secure types of encryption could mean investing in more expensive network hardware that can handle the increased load that this would place upon them.

The original forms of encryption that were used on the internet are no longer secure. With the increase in computing power over the past few decades even a home PC would now be powerful enough to, given enough time, decrypt traffic sent using these early encryption technologies. Modern encryption options are available that cannot be cracked in any reasonable timeframe using existing technology. That is not to say that in 20 years' time the average home computer in whatever form it will then exist, be it desktop, tablet, implant etc, may, thanks to Moore's Law (see Biography on Mr Gordon Moore in chapter 11 for explanation of the term), be powerful enough to decrypt modern encryption. However all is not lost, the expectation is that this security arms race will have produced a more secure form of encryption by this time. That said, it is important to remember that given enough computing power and enough time anything can be decrypted. With modern encryption techniques that would require hundreds of years of existing computing power to decrypt data. Modern encryption is considered secure as after this time frame the value of any such data that is decrypted would, thanks to the amount of time that would have passed, likely be negligible.

The potential impact of quantum computing on security is as yet unknown but could be significant. Traditionally computers work by processing data and requests one bit at a time. If, for example, your PC has a speed of 1 GHz this means that your computer processor can transact one billion instructions per second (Ghz means Giga hertz and Giga means a billion). A 1 GHz dual core processor means that you have two processors each capable of processing one billion instructions per second, so a total of 2 billion instructions per second for your device. It is this type of brute force computing power that allows for older encryption to be broken easily. If you were trying to decrypt a modern encryption algorithm that had a near infinite amount of combinations required to decrypt it, even with a PC with dual core 1Ghz processors capable of a theoretical 2 billion instructions a second it would not be feasible to complete the task in any reasonable length of time. Quantum computing works differently. Instead of trying all possible combinations sequentially it actually tries all possible combinations together at once to give you the result. How this works, at the quantum level, has still not been clearly defined and possible answers range from parallel universes to the vagaries of quantum mechanics. Quantum computing is still in its infancy and is currently more theoretical than practical but has the potential to radically alter the security landscape. Whether and when this will happen will probably not become clear for several more years.

There are two main different types of VPN technologies, client VPN and site to site VPN, and we will take a look at both in some detail.

Client VPN

A remote access or client VPN is the general model that most companies use. Employees can establish a secure connection with the corporate network and access its resources and applications from anywhere in the world that has an available internet connection. This requires the use of client software or certificates and will give the user an experience as if they were physically connected to the corporate office. Microsoft Windows 7 and 8 comes with its own VPN client already installed, but most large companies use corporate client VPN solutions from companies such as HP and Cisco which provide their own dedicated client software.

Companies with a large number of salespeople in the field or business travellers can find such VPNs an ideal solution for their requirements as it will allow them to access and provide private company data over the public internet securely.

Large companies often purchase, deploy, and operate their own remote access VPNs. Smaller organizations can still use VPNs through an enterprise service provider or ESP. Client VPNs have become increasingly popular with people who want more privacy on the internet or who want to get around access controls setup by businesses and governments. A VPN service lets you connect your computer to the Internet through a VPN gateway. The traffic between your PC and this VPN gateway can then be encrypted. That prevents your ISP or your government from easily spying on your data. See chapter 9 for more details on government internet surveillance, but, depending on where you live in the world, all of your internet traffic may be monitored. One consideration here is that encrypting your traffic may only serve to bring you to the attention of the authorities and single you out for special attention.

Some client VPNs services also specialize in getting around access controls—for example a VPN provider may provide a VPN that allows you to connect your device from anywhere in the world to a VPN gateway in the United Kingdom which would allow you to watch television content online that is exclusively for British viewers on the British Broadcasting Corporation's (BBC's) website. This would work as your source IP address would, once you are connected to the VPN, show as coming from a British address, even if you had initiated your connection from Africa. Access control to online services, such as television content, are for often contractual reasons restricted on a country basis by source IP address, and IP addresses are allocated on a geographic basis allowing providers to limit access to services on a country level. See chapter 2 for more detail on IP addressing. These types of services are available online for users, some limited free services are available but performance is normally poor. To get a reliable connection with sufficient bandwidth to fulfil basic requirements such as live streaming of data or acceptable downloads would normally require you to pay a fee to a provider.

When using a client VPN every bit of data you send to the Internet and receive back has to be encrypted and decrypted however with modern computing power this overhead can be easily accommodated with negligible impact on performance.

Site to Site VPN

A site-to-site VPN is a network that allows multiple fixed locations to setup up secure connections over the internet or some other public network infrastructure. It can be used to connect networks to each other, creating an extended and protected network. It essentially extends the network of an organization and makes company resources and applications available to employees in other locations. It uses security protocols in order to encrypt the data and send it through the web. The most common protocol used in site-to-site VPN is IPsec which stands for Internet Protocol Security. Companies that have branches in several locations can use this kind of VPN.

Site-to-site VPNS can be further classified into two types:

Intranet-based VPNs: Companies that have offices in one or more remote locations and want to bring them together through a single private network can set up an intranet VPN, essentially creating a single WAN out of interconnected LANs.

Extranet-based VPNs: This kind of VPN is good for companies that have a close relationship or partnership with other companies, suppliers, or clients. An extranet VPN connects to networks of these companies and allows them to work together in a shared but secure network environment.

The functions of VPN are:

- Data integrity. This ensures that the data broadcasted wasn't altered.
- Access control. It's the function that limits access to the communication channel from unauthorized users.
- Confidentiality. This is the most important part of it

all, by encrypting the data you can be certain that nothing can be copied or read by another entity.

- Authentication. In order for the VPN to be established the authentication, part of which is a password or secret key as it is known in VPN terminology, must match on both ends of the connection.

The main advantages of using a site to site VPN are flexibility and cost. To build a WAN using circuits delivered via an ISP can be expensive; MPLS and point to point circuits can be costly and you may not want to pay for a premium WAN service for a smaller site that has no business critical requirements, e.g. a small sales office. In addition to the cost, traditional dedicated circuits from a WAN provider such as MPLS can have a lead time of up to 90 days in a lot of Western Countries to deliver and activate. With a site to site VPN you can leverage an internet connection, which are generally cheaper, more readily available and usually easier to install. For example, if your site has a phone line in most Western countries you can normally have that phone line activated as an ADSL line within 48 hours and so be online within days instead of months.

To build a site to site VPN you require a device to act as a VPN concentrator. You can get software to install onto a desktop PC or server that can build a tunnel, but the preferred method is to use a network device such as a router that has the required software running on it, a dedicated VPN concentrator or, as is most popular, a firewall (that we will discuss next in this chapter) that has the additional functionality, as most corporate firewalls do, of acting as a VPN gateway. The other end of the connection will also need a device acting as a VPN concentrator, this does not need to be the same type of device, e.g. you can have a Windows server running Microsoft Forefront Threat Management Gateway

(Forefront TMG), previously known as Microsoft Internet Security and Acceleration Server (ISA Server) and on the other end you could have a Cisco router.

A site to site VPN is device independent, it just requires that both ends of the connection have matching parameters such as secret key (password), authentication types (e.g. Internet Protocol Security -IPSEC) and encryption domains (what addresses you are sending through the VPN tunnel).

Firewalls

A consequence of having a device connected to a network is that you may receive unrequested and malicious connection attempts. This is true even on the previously mentioned U.S. DOD's secure SIPRNet—military computers occasionally get viruses like all other computers.

Computer scientists long ago realized that a classical engineering technique could be applied to computers to prevent most types of harmful data. That technique is a firewall.

Engineers, architects, and other design professionals build firewalls to help restrain fires. For example, almost all vehicles have a firewall between the engine compartment and the occupant compartment. If a fire starts in the engine compartment—where it's most likely to start—the firewall will help keep the fire from burning the occupants.

Of course, there are some parts of a vehicle which must pass through the firewall—such as the accelerator and brake pedals (or the wires or tubes in electronic or hydraulic controlled vehicles). So firewalls aren't just barriers—they're barriers which let through the expected good things and block the unexpected bad things.

Network firewalls operate on the same principle. The firewall can be hardware or a software system. It basically prevents unauthorized access to or from a network. All data sent and received through a firewall is analysed often packet per packet and anything that doesn't meet the security criteria is blocked. It can protect your computer or network from viruses, hackers, worms and bugs while controlling incoming and out coming traffic.

Simple firewalls keep track of all the requests you send out to the Internet; when a computer on the Internet responds to one of those requests, the firewall lets the response go back through the firewall to your device. This is the type of firewall normally built into home and small business routers.

When your firewall receives data which you didn't request, it simply ignores it. This is an effective technique at keeping out most basic attacks.

The minimum security policy you should apply on a firewall is to allow all outbound traffic i.e. any traffic initiated from your internal network but to deny all inbound traffic, all traffic initiated from the outside of your firewall, usually the internet.

There are two main types of firewall, hardware and software firewalls.

Hardware Firewalls

You will find hardware Firewalls normally at the network edge between most organisations networks and the internet. It is important to secure your network to ensure that all external connections, e.g. if you have any internet connections or connections to third parties all this traffic should be routed through a firewall.

Hardware Firewalls come in a variety of forms, some routers have firewall functionality built in. There are dedicated hardware firewalls provided by companies such as Cisco (with their Adaptive Security Appliances – known as ASA) and Fortinet (with their Fortigate devices) which offer additional functionality. Early firewalls worked primarily on the network layer, layer 3 and below, so they controlled access via IP address. Modern firewalls now work on all layers, from the physical to the Application layer. They are able to scan traffic passing through them and look for malicious content such as viruses, malware or any behaviour that is considered suspicious. Protecting your traffic on your gateway in this manner reduces the risks of viruses and malware getting into your corporate LAN and onto your key systems and user devices.

Most home users getting an ADSL service from their local ISP will have a router that comes with some built in firewall functionality. This built in firewall will normally be configured by default to not allow inbound connections to any hosts on the internal network. For home users this is normally sufficient. It is only normally organisations that have multiple devices that would use a dedicated hardware firewall.

Good security is about defence in depth and not having a single point of failure. Having a hardware firewall is not a replacement for individual firewalls on all devices. Every windows based device should have a software firewall on it.

Software Firewalls

Software firewalls are programs that can be installed on an individual computer that may or may not be connected to a network. They are designed to distinguish between programs so; they can allow or deny certain connections and allow or deny internet access from certain installed programs as desired or appropriate.

This type of firewall is normally designed to be user friendly, but will only protect the computer on which is installed, so if you have more computers you will, depending on which client software you use, have to buy more than one license and configure them on every device. The up side is that you can easily determine the level of protection and there is higher flexibility, the user or administrator decides which applications should be allowed or not. Probably the best feature is that it's portable; once installed on a computer it works no matter where the computer is, whether it's on the office LAN, the coffee shop Wi-Fi network or the user's home network.

The down side of software firewalls is that it utilizes more resources and, depending on the performance specifications of your computer and how many security features you have enabled this may impact the systems performance.

Microsoft Windows 7 and 8 come with a built in software firewall, called Microsoft firewall, which is enabled by default. This is a good software firewall that is adequate for most users and small companies.

Please see chapter 7 for more details on security topics but in short a PC should also be configured with antivirus software as well as a firewall. Anti-malware and anti-spyware software is optional but recommended for any users who may be exposed to the darker sides of the internet.

Different types of firewall have their advantages, the hardware firewall checks every single package that goes into the network, but the software firewall has the ability to check the computer or device constantly. A secure network would have a hardware firewall deployed at the network edge and would have all host devices running their own software firewall and antivirus software.

Chapter 5

Wireless and Mobile Connectivity

Everything You Need to Know About Wireless Networks in Plain English

Getting online looks vastly different than it did a little over a decade ago. Rather than sitting at a desk, listening to the hum of the bulky desktop computer and the screech of the dial-up connection, you now connect to the Internet with devices large and small, anytime and anywhere. Do you have a hankering to read *The New York Times* before leaving your bed in the morning? No problem. Want to share the mockup of the new web design during your staff meeting? Shove your laptop in your case and go. Need to finish the homework for your online class while you're waiting at the bus stop? Log on and write that essay. Thanks to wireless and mobile networks, you are no longer confined to a designated workspace despite living in a highly connected world. But what is a wireless network, exactly, and how are they different from wired connections? What are the benefits of going wireless and where can hotspots be found? What are the different types of wireless connections and the pros and cons of each? Finally, are there any health risks to be aware of regarding using these networks? This guide will tell you all that and more.

What is a wireless network?

We've all heard the term, but what is a wireless network? Simply put, a wireless network is a network that links two or more devices to each other and also normally the Internet over a short distance using radio waves. These WLANs (Wireless Local Area Networks) are used to maintain communications between computers and devices. Desktops with wireless capabilities, laptops, tablets, printers, smartphones, MP3 players and other devices can all use wireless networks. Most wireless network routers — the piece of equipment that transmits the wireless signal — have a range of approximately 100-300 feet. Businesses that offer free Wi-Fi to their patrons usually have a number of routers and access points to provide coverage to all areas of the establishment.

A wireless personal area network (WPAN) is a term used for devices connected wirelessly within reach of a single person. An example of this is if you have a Bluetooth headset connected to your phone, this is a WPAN.

A wireless metropolitan area network (WMAN) is a wireless network that connects multiple different Wireless Local Area Networks (WLANs).

How are wireless networks different from wired networks?

Unlike a wired network, wireless networks do not use cables to provide Internet access to devices. Wired connections use cables, most commonly Ethernet, to connect to a router or switch at one end and an end user device at the other. Wired connections have traditionally been faster than wireless connections, but recent advances in wireless technology have bridged this gap to render it almost nonexistent. Wired connections were also favoured over wireless connections because the latter were susceptible to interference from other devices, but this is not the case with the newest Wi-Fi standards, as is explained later in this chapter. Wireless networks are fast becoming the preference of most home and business users due to the many benefits a wireless connection provides.

What are the benefits of a wireless connection?

For years, the use of wireless networks has grown to the point where it is now an everyday practice to fire up any number of devices to connect to the Internet wirelessly. A wireless network is convenient. You can access the Internet anytime, anywhere, from any Wi-Fi enabled device as long as you're within the network's range. Wi-Fi offers mobility so that workers and students are no longer stuck at their desks while working. Being able to take computers and other mobile devices anywhere encourages collaboration in the work environment. And those are just the benefits for the end user.

For the home or business implementing a wireless network, it is much easier to set up than a wired network that may require extensive use of wires and cables to get all devices working properly. Wi-Fi networks are more easily expandable because they don't require buildings to be rewired or new cables to be added to already crowded work areas. Wireless networks have become increasingly secure, so there is now no worry about anyone accessing protected data as long as you have the correct security measures in place. Wireless networks are less expensive and quicker to install because you avoid the costs and delays associated with the wiring, installation of cables and the time to set up a complicated network. For these same reasons a wireless network is more flexible as it can be more easily expanded than its wired counterpart. In some locations, if your building is listed or if you have an uncooperative landlord, the running of network cables may not be permissible so a wireless network gives you a viable alternative.

Where are wireless networks used?

Wireless networks are used in a number of businesses and public spaces nowadays. Have you ever connected to the internet at a restaurant, airport or in the library using Wi-Fi? If so, you were utilizing that establishment's Wi-Fi. The use of these networks has become increasingly common in order to provide an enhanced user experience to clients and customers. Wi-Fi is offered in many cafés, airports, hotels and government facilities. College campuses offer wireless connections via their Campus Area Networks (CANs) to students to enable them to connect to their laptops and other mobile devices anytime, anywhere. Even churches have begun offering Wi-Fi hotspots for churchgoers to follow along in the Bible on their mobile devices. Most business and public Wi-Fi hotspots are free to use, but some require a subscription. Most hotels and even cruise ships nowadays provide Wi-Fi for their patrons, but often at an additional cost.

What are the different types of wireless networks?

The Institute for Electrical and Electronics Engineers (IEEE) has established 802.11 as the Wi-Fi standard. It was named 802.11 after the group that oversaw its development, but since that name wasn't very marketable, it was dubbed "Wi-Fi" to make it catchier. There are several different types of 802.11 wireless networks, which we will examine in detail. Please note that the speeds and coverage distances stated here are theoretical. These are really up to speeds and in the real world performance will rarely, if ever, achieve these theoretical maximums.

802.11b

Because the original 802.11 technology was too slow with speeds only reaching up to 2 Mbit/s, updated protocols called 802.11b and 802.11a were developed. The 802.11b technology caught on much faster and was cheaper to implement. This type of protocol offers speeds of up to 11 megabits per second (Mbit/s). Its range varies from approximately 150 – 300 feet. When compared to the other wireless protocols, 802.11b is slow, doesn't accommodate many users and is susceptible to interference from microwaves, cordless phones and other appliances that run on the 2.4 GHz frequency. This protocol was more frequently used in homes, which require smaller networks than businesses. This protocol was officially released in 1999 and is now no longer in widespread use as it has been superseded by superior protocols.

802.11a

Both 802.11a and 802.11b were developed at the same time, but 802.11a was slower to catch on. It is much faster than its more popular counterpart with speeds of up to 54Mbit/s. This protocol runs on a 5.0 GHz frequency, so it is more resistant to interference than 802.11b. Unfortunately, it also has a shorter signal range of only 100-300 feet, requiring several access points to offer more coverage. Because these signals operate at higher frequencies, they have difficulty penetrating walls and other obstructions between the router and the end user. For businesses and large organizations, 802.11a technology was a better fit due to its faster speeds, ability to handle more users and lack of interference from other devices. This protocol was officially released in 1999 at the same time as 802.11b but never gained widespread market share. As with 802.11b it is no longer in widespread use as it has been superseded by superior protocols.

802.11g

A new standard was developed in 2002 called 802.11g. It combined the speed of 802.11a with the wide range of 802.11b. This standard offers speeds up to 54 Mbit/s and is not easily obstructed. It is backwards compatible with 802.11b technology, but allows for more simultaneous users to access the connection. Unfortunately, it too operates on the 2.4 GHz frequency and is susceptible to interference. This protocol was superseded by 802.11n so is no longer in widespread use, at least it is not the protocol of choice for new devices being sold onto the market.

802.11n

The 802.11n standard is the most popular and widely used protocol during 2014. The speed of this protocol depends on the number of data streams that the hardware supports, but can range from up to 54 – 600 Mbit/s, a stark improvement over older technologies. It uses multiple signals and antennas to provide lightning fast speeds. It, too, can accommodate a greater number of users and boasts the widest range. The signal is not easily obstructed and resists interference from other devices because it can operate on both 2.4 and 5.0 GHz frequencies. When used on the 2.4 GHz frequency, it is backwards compatible with 802.11g equipment but experiences the same problems with interference.

802.11ac

The 802.11ac protocol is an up and coming technology with faster speeds and longer ranges than its 802.11n predecessor. It is sometimes called 5G as it operates at the 5 GHz frequency. It is up to three times faster than 802.11n and because of its incredibly fast speeds it is also referred to as Gig Wi-Fi. It is now widely supported on new devices and has the advantage of being backwards compatible with 802.11n. It is an ideal choice for streaming media, gaming and transferring data. If you're considering an 802.11ac router, make sure it's backwards compatible as a lot of existing devices you may own or have to support, such as mobile phones or laptops may not support this newer protocol.

802.11ad

This wireless standard was adopted by the IEEE in early 2013 and boasts speeds of up to 7 Gbit/s over 60 GHz frequencies. This is often referred to as Wi-Gig. Instead of replacing current wireless network technology as 802.11ac intends to do, 802.11ad is meant to complement it. It will work best by providing direct links between devices that are close to each other because, at its extremely high 60 GHz frequency, it is unable to penetrate walls and other obstructions. This is because the higher the frequency the shorter the wavelength which means higher attenuation and a shorter overall range. This 802.11ad Wi-Gig has an effective range of only about 10 metres.

What is WiMAX?

WiMAX stands for the Worldwide Interoperability for Microwave Access. Just as Wi-Fi refers to 802.11 standards, WiMAX refers to 802.16 standards. This protocol is designed to deliver speeds of 30-40 Mbit/s on average, but up to 1 Gbit for fixed stations. It is dubbed by some technology experts as "Wi-Fi on steroids" and can provide broadband connections, cellular backhaul and hotspots, just as Wi-Fi does. The advantage of WiMAX, though is that it can be used at greater distances without deploying fibre optic or DSL networks. It can provide broadband access to entire cities with a range of up to 30 miles for each fixed station and 3-10 miles for each mobile station whereas Wi-Fi is limited to 100-300 feet. WiMAX is currently being used in rural areas and emerging markets in an effort to reduce costs associated with cable, fibre and DSL. The downside to WiMAX is that it is much more expensive when compared to 802.11 wireless technologies.

How is data protected on wireless networks?

One reason that so many institutions and organizations were initially reluctant to go wireless was because these wireless networks were deemed less secure than wired networks. Today so long as you use and correctly implement the right type of encryption this is no longer the case. Let's take a look at the different types of encryption and determine which is the safest for your home or office.

WEP

Wired Equivalent Privacy (WEP) is a security algorithm first established in the late 1990s to protect data as it is shared over wireless networks. It encrypts data sent over the network from one computer to another. Unfortunately, this protocol had many security weaknesses and was easy to crack. It is still in use today to support older devices that are not capable of WPA or higher, but is not recommended for use.

WPA

Wi-Fi Protected Access (WPA) was designed as a more secure replacement for WEP. With this protocol, data is encrypted and security keys are checked to ensure they have not been modified. WPA authenticates users to allow only those who are authorized to be on the network. This protocol works with most network adaptors but may not work with old routers or access points.

WPA2

WPA2 is the current security protocol recommended for both homes and businesses. It offers government grade data protection and is extremely difficult to hack. All Wi-Fi CERTIFIED products use WPA2. This protocol is much more secure but may not work with old network adaptors and devices. There are two types of WPA2: WPA2-PSK and WPA2-ENT. The WPA2-PSK (Pre-Shared Key) is used most often for homes and small businesses. Each wireless device uses the same 256-bit security key to authenticate itself on the network. These passphrases are stored locally and are vulnerable to being taken by others. For that reason, PSK is not recommended in the business environment. WPA2-ENT (Enterprise) is used for large business networks. New encryption keys are created each time a user logs on to the network, and the passphrases are not stored locally.

Bluetooth

Bluetooth is a protocol (IEEE 802.15.1) for the use of low-power radio communications to connect different personal consumer devices such as phones, computers, headsets and other network devices over short distances wirelessly. The name Bluetooth is the Anglicized name derived from Harald Bluetooth, a 10th century king in Denmark who had a reputation for being able to get different people to communicate.

Wireless signals transmitted with Bluetooth cover comparatively short distances, typically up to 10 metres (30 feet). Bluetooth devices generally communicate at speeds of less than 1 Mbit/s[106]. As it's a relatively low powered technology dedicated Bluetooth devices often have a long battery life.

Bluetooth networks operate in a Wireless Personal Area Network (WPAN) which was covered earlier in this chapter. A piconet is the name for a network that is created using wireless Bluetooth connections. Bluetooth operates in a master-slave setup with a minimum of two and a maximum of eight Bluetooth connected devices. You would always have a single master device with the remainder - 1 to a maximum of 7 other Bluetooth devices in a single piconet - being slaves.

Due to the limited range, the restricted number of devices that can be in a piconet and its comparatively slow speeds and limited security Bluetooth technology is not a suitable replacement for Wi-Fi[107].

What are the health risks associated with wireless networks?

Speculation about the health risks associated with the use of wireless networks led to unfounded fear among people about this technology causing memory loss and other types of brain damage. The claims about memory loss and other health risks have not been validated scientifically. The Health Protection Agency in the United Kingdom has refuted these claims, stating that radio frequency exposure from Wi-Fi signals is much lower than what people are exposed to from their mobile phones. Wi-Fi signals are only sent intermittently whereas cell phones send out continuous radio frequencies. In fact, Wi-Fi runs on approximately the same frequency as microwave ovens, but at lower power. If you feel safe using a microwave or cell phone, you should feel even safer utilizing wireless networks.

Wi-Fi networks now saturate developed parts of the world and wireless networking is expected to continue growing in popularity, speed, security and accessibility. As mobile devices begin to overtake desktops and laptops for connecting to the Internet, high speed, low-cost networks will become the norm for communicating between both people and devices. By understanding what these networks are and how they work, you can make informed decisions about installing or upgrading your own wireless networking equipment.

Chapter 6

Cloud Computing

Cloud Computing- The Past, the Present and the Future

Cloud computing has become ubiquitous in the last few years, but what does this generic term actually mean? In this detailed look at Cloud Computing, we look at what it is, how it began, and what the future holds.

What is cloud computing?

The cloud is the internet. It is not a single physical thing but rather in other words a network of servers. Lots of these servers are setup and operated by different companies in different locations offering different services. Cloud computing is a non-technical term for cloud technology and services. Its exact definition may vary with usage, but it is generally used to describe the concept of the cloud and everything about it. Contrary to what some may believe, there is no universal technical definition for it.

Considering the ambiguity of cloud computing, it could refer to cloud storage, cloud hosting services, and other concopts and services in which a group of devices are connected with each other through a real-time communication network. These devices could include scanners, desktop computers, laptops, and, more recently, tablet PCs and mobile phones.

By becoming part of a network, a device can essentially use the combined resources of the other connected devices. Thus, the local device does not have to take on the entire workload for running cloud applications. The hardware and software requirements for running applications decrease, allowing the end user to do more with their local machine.

For instance, cloud storage services allow end users to store their data on a server network instead of or in addition to their local device. Similarly, cloud-based software runs from the vendor's server network and only uses a fraction of the end user's local device resources when compared to running entirely locally.

One of the most successful examples of a cloud based service is Facebook. All information is held centrally by Facebook in their vast data centres and users login and just view their data through their app or browser. When a user logs into Facebook and they see data on their display this information that they are viewing is not held locally but rather their display is a window through which they look at the data held in the cloud.

Cloud computing- a history

The history of cloud computing can be traced back to the beginning of the internet. Back in the 1960s, the concept of a global network of computers was introduced by J.C. R. Licklider. His concept of an Intergalactic Computer Network described most of what the internet is today. He also played a key role in the development of ARPANET, the first

TCP/IP network that was the predecessor of the modern internet.

The concept of sharing and delivering computer resources through a network also began during the same period. While some say Licklider introduced the concept for the first time, others attribute this to John McCarthy, who proposed computation power being delivered like a public utility.

Since the establishment of ARPANET in 1969, cloud computing and internet have developed almost parallel to each other. However, what most people understand as cloud computing is the most recent evolution of the concept that began with Web 2.0. This is because the term 'cloud' has only become popular recently, with bigger and better cloud services being offered.

Although cloud computing is as old as the internet itself, one of its first major milestones was the establishment of Salesforce.com. Introduced in 1999, Salesforce.com delivered enterprise applications through the internet. By 2009, Web 2.0 hit the mainstream and large organizations like Google began offering enterprise applications straight from the browser.

How is cloud computing used today?

Cloud computing hit its stride in the late 1990s when available bandwidth for internet connectivity increased significantly. Today, ready availability of bandwidth and the ability of almost any device to connect to the internet has given cloud computing a wider scope.

Here is a look at how cloud computing is used today:

Online backup
Online backup is a form of remote data storage where you

back up files and folders from your local device to the cloud. All the selected content present in the local machine's hard disk is regularly synced and backed up on the server through an internet connection. By doing so, the end user always has two copies of his/her data- one on the local hard drive and the other on a remote server network.

Why create two copies of the same data and store it remotely? The reason is simple- local hard drives are more prone to loss, theft, fire, or other disasters that make the files in them unusable. By storing the same data on a remote server and keeping it synchronized with the local hard drive, the user will not lose any data even when the locally stored data is corrupted or eliminated.

Companies that offer online backup services own and manage their own data servers and automatically copy the consumer's selected files in these servers. While this basic concept remains the same, other aspects like the amount of backup storage allowed and the speed of syncing data varies. Two of the leading companies in the online backup world are Carbonite and Idrive.

Online storage
Online storage, network storage, or online data storage is a method of storing data on a network server connected through the internet. Instead of saving data on a hard drive or physical storage device, the consumer stores it in the cloud. This data can then be accessed or downloaded at any time through the consumer's online account.

Like online backup, online storage also helps keep a person's data safe and secure. However, online storage services do not normally sync all data on a device or the device itself. Instead, most modern online storage providers set up a separate folder on the consumer's local machine. The consumer can then upload data on the cloud by copying it into this local folder. Alternatively, they could also upload and access this data through an internet browser.

A customer's online storage account can be accessed and downloaded from several devices, and people can share their files with others online too. This is different from online backup, where data from just one local machine is uploaded and regularly synced. Thus, online storage is a better collaboration tool. Different people can access common files, work on them, and others can view the results in real time.

Online storage can also act as a form of online backup as you will normally hold one copy locally and there will be another copy of the data held online in the cloud. The leading companies in the online storage world are Dropbox and Google.

Disaster Recovery
One of the key benefits of using the cloud is the protection it gives an organization in the event of a disaster. Should a flood, fire or other disaster strike a business's premises all data held in that location could be lost. A lot of businesses backup data to tape which are then held offsite at a secure location. This secure location has to be far enough away so it is not impacted by the same disaster that impacted the main site but close enough so that the backup data can be accessible. Recovering systems from tape can be a lengthy process and backup tape failure rates are estimated at 15%.

If your data is held online then you can access the data from anywhere you have an internet connection. You are reliant on your cloud provider keeping your data secure. Most of the bigger players in the industry have multiple locations where your data is held to provide a reliable, resilient service. Before choosing a provider it is best to verify the size and scale of the company to ensure that you placing your data with an established provider that is not likely to go out of business.

Email- One of the first and most common cloud-based services

Electronic mails were exchanged through local networks even before the development of the internet. In fact, it became a crucial tool for creating the internet. The modern form of online email as most people know it can, once again, be traced back to ARPANET.

Global online email is a cloud service. A user uses the resources of a host to create and send an email. These hosts exchange messages using SMTP (Simple Mail Transfer Protocol) over the internet.

Gmail, Hotmail, and other free email hosts

Gmail, Hotmail, and Yahoo! Mail are examples of web-based email services. This type of email allows users to sign into their email account from a web browser. They can then send and receive emails. The service providers use their own network of servers to store and send emails and attachments. End users can access their email account through local computers and mobile devices using dedicated applications as well. For instance, Microsoft Outlook on Windows PCs allows users to access their accounts through POP and IMAP servers and download a copy of their emails locally. Ordinarily when accessing your email through a web browser your data you are just viewing a copy of the data which is held in the cloud.

Exchange servers for big businesses

Exchange servers are email-based communications servers running Microsoft Exchange email server software for big businesses, other software by other companies is available but Microsoft Exchange is the market leader. Companies can purchase licenses for using these servers for their business emails from Microsoft and authorized resellers. If a company has a server running Microsoft Exchange it can host its own email service, just like Hotmail and Gmail, but instead of the email address being name@gmail.com it would be name@yourcompanydomainname.com.

Most exchange servers are configured to run on the internet to allow users of the company to access their exchange email accounts remotely e.g. from a web browser on their computer or via their mobile phones.

Cloud computing delivery

In order to understand how modern cloud computing services are delivered, let's split it into two parts- the front and back end. Both these parts are connected through the internet or some other network. The front end is what the end user sees and uses. The back end is considered by most people to be the cloud section.

The front end includes the local device and application used by the end user and the interface designed by the service provider. The application could be a web browser or a dedicated app on a mobile phone, and the interface can vary with each service provider.

The back end includes the network of servers and storage devices that form the 'cloud'. This is the basic architecture of every cloud computing system, but the delivery of the service can be done in different ways.

Here is a look at three common types of cloud service delivery:

SaaS (software as a service)
In this form of cloud service delivery, the end user is able to access application software through the cloud while the service provider manages the infrastructure needed to run

the software. Also known as software on demand, the payment model for SaaS is commonly decided on a pay-per-usage basis. Most cloud-based SaaS providers ask for a monthly or yearly subscription fee for access to their software. Salesforce.com is one of the earliest forms of SaaS. Microsoft Office 365 is another modern example of SaaS.

SaaS as a cloud service model offers several advantages to both the end user and vendor. For the end user, it lowers the cost of service and burden on their system. This is especially useful for businesses. Their IT costs are reduced and they only need to pay for what they use. There is no overhead associated with implementing, installing, and maintaining the software.

The zero implementation and maintenance requirements also save time for end user and allows for a faster deployment to their users when compared to standing up their own infrastructure. If the end user is a business, this means more time for core business functions instead of IT maintenance.

HaaS (Hardware as a Service)
Hardware as a Service or HaaS is another pay-for-usage model of cloud service delivery. In this case, the end user accesses the processing power and infrastructure of the service provider for a fee. It is essentially a form of grid computing, where several computers work in sync with each other and act as a single powerful computer.

The service provider here sells access to their grid to users for a fee. The user typically sends the data over the service provider, who processes the data using the grip and returns the result. Google Compute Engine is another recent example of a HaaS product, although it is restricted only to Linux users.

UCaaS (Unified Communication as a Service)

Unified Communications includes real-time and non-real-time communication services. Examples of real-time communication includes instant messaging, VoIP, video conferencing, data sharing through whiteboards, and call control. Non-real-time communications include email, SMS, and voicemail. Thus, UCaaS is a set of communication products provided through a single unified user interface across multiple devices.

UCaaS is a cloud service delivery model in which Unified Communications are delivered by a service provider over the internet or some other IP network. Enterprise-level communication technology, video conferencing and telephony services, and online conferencing programs are delivered through this model. Small businesses are the biggest beneficiaries of this delivery model because they can avoid the installation and operation costs associated with deploying a complete Unified Communication solution locally.

The future of cloud computing

Cloud computing is an old concept, but it has grown exponentially in importance in a very short time. Advancements in networking and mobile technology have made the internet faster and more accessible, and this has increased the scope of cloud computing applications. For many, it is the next wave of IT and the future of data storage and usage.

Cloud computing has inspired radical innovations and new business models and the majority of internet users use the cloud in some way or another.

Of course, cloud computing is not without its concerns. Two of the major concerns are with data security and privacy. There are still many people and companies that worry about handing over important data to another organization. Some governments restrict any confidential information of designated levels of security classification being stored in a cloud style environment as they know it is not completely secure.

This issue of data security and privacy received additional focus in 2013 with the revelations from the former US I.T. worker Mr Edward Snowden. He revealed how Western governments routinely intercept and access information either in transit on the internet (intercepting and interrogating in real time data on international and national ISP circuits within and into and out of their own countries) or held by internet companies such as Facebook, Microsoft and Google. Mr Snowden also claimed that the US government had direct access to the servers of these companies, something the companies have denied although due to the volume of information the US government is acknowledged to be receiving from these companies some form of direct connection would be expected.

Such are the benefits of cloud computing, such as accessing your data anywhere at any time, having full access to your emails, having a centralized source for data, having a secure offsite backup of your data, leveraging the cloud services, etc., that most companies and individuals are willing to accept and where possible try and mitigate the security concerns in return for the services and functionality on offer. These services and this functionality would not all be available without some sort of compromise.

Stronger security measures, a better use of security technology and a greater understanding of what information is being intercepted and accessed by governments can be expected in the future. With the continued move towards more mobile devices for accessing the internet and with internet bandwidth speeds increasing globally every year cloud computing is not only here to stay but will continue to proliferate.

Chapter 7

Online Security

"There are risks and costs to a program of action--but they are far less than the long range cost of comfortable inaction. — John F. Kennedy"

This quote by John F Kennedy is a suitable opening for a chapter that deals with a ubiquitous topic- Network security and the measures one can take to avoid compromising sensitive data and information. We are at a juncture where it is impossible to isolate oneself from the internet and the other myriad networks that we are forced to be a part of. Every day we surf the World Wide Web in order to:

1. Procure information
2. Complete tasks
3. Initiate transactions

The internet is a teeming virtual landscape of a billion plus users and it is obviously a proposition not without risk to allow personal and professional information to travel its lanes often unprotected. IBM reports that in the **United States alone in 2013 there has been a 38% increase in the reported instances of loss, theft and appropriation** of personal information as compared to 2012. That is alarming. Moreover **59% of respondents from a survey on security considerations declared that they will vastly increase their budget for internet safety measures over the next 12 months.**

To understand what the brouhaha is about, a cognizance of the real scenario behind these reports is needed. As is the realization that in this particular case "comfortable inaction" can cause severe and sometimes crippling financial losses.

Networks and Risks

A network is an interconnected system of devices (also called nodes) such that data can travel from one node to another with the help of interconnecting media like cables and wires. To understand how a node in a network can be at risk, it is important to know how a network functions.

A basic network is made up of the following components:

1. Nodes (Processing devices like CPUs or Output devices)
2. NIC or Network Interface Controller
3. Switches/Routers
4. Interconnecting medium
5. Server

The cornerstone of a network is the client-server relationship. A server is a powerful machine or a collection of machines capable of fulfilling/processing the requests sent in by the client machines (nodes). Each client (node) is installed with a NIC that allows it to connect to a switch with the help of cables/optical fibres (interconnecting medium). The switch or, in some cases, the router sends the requests initiated by the client or the data packets sent by the server in response to the correct dcctination. From this simple explanation itself we can identify one fact: **There is information constantly travelling through a network and if by any means it falls into the hands of a 3rd party, it can be used to extract privileged information about an individual or an organization.** Now consider the case of the internet which has billions of nodes and devices buzzing with data. The spread of the net is worldwide and without stringent security measures it is sometimes very easy to spy upon the "communication" between two nodes. Data is vulnerable throughout the transit period and even when stored in nodes.

Potentially the entry points to a network are most susceptible to security breaches. But that is not the final word. From time to time UPnP (Universal Plug and Play), a component which is used to increase and enhance the visibility of devices like printers and routers within a network, too has been accused of putting data at risk. Thus a number of weak points or flaws within a network can facilitate data breach and loss if protection measures are not up to date. **Online transactions aren't the only means of inviting security threats. The information stored on a computer, which is never disclosed on the net, may be open to a host of fraudulent entities.**

The Different Network Risks

What is vulnerability?
In the terminology of computing, a "vulnerability" is a flaw that allows an attacker to somehow compromise the integrity of a network and degrade its information security capacity. Vulnerability management is thus a cyclic process of continuous identifying, classifying and remediating vulnerabilities to make a system reinforced. **Network security is a part of data vulnerability management and refers specifically to measures that can mitigate risks to the network and the data travelling through it.**

According to IT security the following are the ten biggest threats to the reliability and integrity of a network:

1. Viruses and Worms
2. Trojan Horses
3. Zombie computers and bots
4. Phishing
5. Packet Sniffers
6. Maliciously coded websites
7. Password Attacks
8. Hardware loss and residual data fragments
9. Shared computers
10. SPAM

Viruses and worms are the bane of internet and network security and are addressed in detail later in the chapter.

Trojan Horses
A "Trojan Horse" is described as a malicious piece of coding that is hidden in an innocuous program like software to be downloaded from a website. It can get installed with the apparently harmless code and wreak havoc on the host computer, tampering with the file allocation table (FAT)[108] and crippling the capacity of the computer or node to interact and communicate with others within a network.

Zombie Computers and Botnets
A zombie computer is a node that has been infiltrated by a hacker in a clever manner such that the owner is unaware of the corruption. The hacker accomplishes this with specialized tools and can at will control the operations of the node. It can be used to send out SPAM or attack other web pages thus incriminating the original user of illegal activities. This is increasingly used by terrorists to cover their tracks and shift the focus of any ensuing investigation to innocent citizens. A Botnet is a collection of such

controlled nodes

Phishing
This is a threat to a network's security posed by a non-technical attack. It can take many forms. Often in case of phishing, mails soliciting confidential information are sent to the victims under the guise of a respectable organization or company. The disseminated information is then used to steal the identity of the victims or to hack into accounts like PayPal where money may be stored or credit cards synced. Other times the fraudster will make a phone call impersonating the victim or pretending to be a legitimate authority to gain illegitimate access or information.

Packet Sniffers
Packet sniffers are devices or programs which allow unscrupulous individuals to eavesdrop on the communication taking place between two or more nodes on a network. The information gathered is then analysed later to learn privileged information or to build up a profile of a user for identity thefts.

Maliciously Coded Websites
These websites are purposely or structurally infected. Their sole purpose is to install malicious programs or bits of code in the computer of the site visitor to either crash the node or to steal sensitive, confidential information. According to a report issued by AVG, almost 300,000 maliciously coded infected sites appear on the internet every day! These malicious websites generally use well known exploits of Microsoft Windows operating systems or internet browsers. A good way to protect against these type of attacks is to ensure that if you are using a Windows based computer that all available Windows updates have been installed on your system.

Password Attacks
Generally most restricted areas of a network need the

users to input passwords to gain access. This can be anything from a simple log in into a computer to bank account passwords which are stored and remembered by either by the browser or devices used to access the account. A password attack is an attack launched by a cyber-criminal to gain possession of the passwords, this may be by use of a password cracking program.

Hardware Loss and Residual Data Fragments
More than 10 million identity threats each year occur because of hardware loss and residual data fragments. If a hardware device like a laptop or a mobile phone is stolen, and the important files are not properly encrypted, it can open a vista of opportunities for the criminally inclined. More than individuals, large companies and their executive officers are at threat from this risk. Old files and residual data (which is not wiped out even if you delete files) can be recovered by hackers to blackmail organizations or sell sensitive information to competitors. But despite the looming problems, in the USA in a report commissioned in 2013 it found that only 12% of companies employ encryption.

Shared Computers
A single node which can be handled and accessed by several users is obviously at risk. Even if each user has a separate account and can't log in to the Admin section of the device. Carelessness on the part of one user can allow another user to read, download and even tamper with information not intended for the eyes of others outside the circle of trust.

SPAM
The full form of SPAM is Sales, Promotion and Advertising Mails. A SPAM campaign consists of a flood of unwanted messages which are delivered en masse to multiple e-mail addresses irrespective of the interest or the lack of it on part of the user for the contents of the mail. Though not

strictly harmful in their own right, SPAM messages are irritating and can have links to maliciously coded websites or programs with "Trojan Horses". It has been widely reported that 90% of all emails sent are actually SPAM.

Basic Network Security and Best Practices

Where there is darkness, there is often light. And with these seemingly endless threats to the security of devices logged to a network there are sophisticated solutions which can be implemented to mitigate the risk and ensure the safety of data and confidentiality of information.

What is device hardening?
Hardening of a device refers to elimination of security vulnerabilities or their mitigation to ensure reinforcement of a network. Hardening should be done on a priority basis for servers, workstations and network devices such as firewalls, switches and routers. Hardening can be achieved in two ways.

1. **Remediation**- A software upgrade
2. **Mitigation**- Changing the configuration settings

Some of the measures that can be implemented in order to protect data and the integrity of nodes in a network are:

1. **Use of strong passwords**- Password attacks are very common and easily implemented because password crackers are found online! In order to protect either sensitive data or to prevent trespassing of "confidential" virtual territory by 3rd party entities, passwords need to be extremely robust and difficult to guess. Ideally, according to Microsoft a password should be 8 to 12 characters in length, a balanced combination of upper and lower case characters, numerals and special signs like the ampersand. **Strong passwords can to a**

large extent prevent password related attacks as more complicated ones will take a very long time to crack.

2. **Use of firewalls**- A firewall is a system which is capable of scrutinizing messages, requests or packets entering a private network from the internet so that only those which comply with the security specifications of the network in question are granted access. As per the client- server relationship, in networks a large number of requests and data packets are exchanged back and forth. With a strong firewall in place to harden the network, harmful content can never be allowed to breach the security of an intranet (one that is private and not accessible to external agents). A firewall is best implemented as a combination of software and hardware solutions. The most common firewall techniques are:

   • Packet Filtering- Scrutinizing of packets entering and leaving the intranet
   • Application gateway- Employs security and hardening measures to data transfer and remote control protocols like FTP (File Transfer Protocol)[109] and Telnet[110]

   A firewall is more of a preventive measure than a cure which an anti-virus is.

3. **Usage of effective anti-virus**- Most anti-virus programs are anti-spyware and malware too. When installed on a particular node it can efficiently identify and destroy existing viruses as well as incoming threats to the node by means of maliciously coded websites and bad links in SPAM mails. **Anti-viruses can identify zombie computers, terminate viruses/malware/spyware and also get rid of Trojan Horses. Some have an option for a "Site Advisor" which can warn users when visiting a site that can be potentially harmful. As discussed later in this**

chapter, installing anti-spyware is good practice.

4. **Constant update**- There are hundreds of new viruses and spyware generated each day and it is extremely important to keep network security measures updated. A virus database of an anti-virus software solution is updated almost constantly and it is imperative that the "Update Enable" option be checked. Security configurations may also need to be reset from time to time in order to ensure complete protection.

5. **Laptop and mobile phone encryption- In order to combat the threat of hardware loss and residual data fragments**, both portable devices-laptops and mobile phones need to be encrypted so that the information can't be accessed or read without a password. Remote wiping wherein a lost device can be completely wiped of any data needs to be in place as well.

These simple solutions and practices when properly used can eliminate most of the common data security issues.

MEASURE	PREVENTION AGAINST
Use of strong passwords	Password related attacks
Use of firewalls	Against packet sniffing, viruses, bots and all suspicious connections to a private network/intranet
Use of strong anti-virus	Viruses, bots, worms, Trojan Horses, maliciously coded websites and bad links in phishing attempts.
Regular updates	Most security related exploits
Data encryption and remote wiping	Loss of hardware and residual data fragments

Viruses, Worms and Spyware

Viruses and worms are not organic life forms as the name suggests. They are the most dominant security threats to the structure and the ability of a network to keep data protected and uncompromised.

What are Viruses and Worms?

Both viruses and worms are bits of harmful or malicious code (malcode) referred to as malware in short. They can cause a large number of adverse side effects which can be a simple slowing down of the operating system or a complete crash of the hard disk and all associated programs.

A virus is almost always cleverly hidden in an .exe file. The hapless user may download an executable file from the internet and run the program in his machine. This unleashes the virus which is then capable of inserting a duplicate or a copy of itself in the files, programs, or applications it is meant to target and corrupt or destroy them.

A worm is similar to a virus in the sense that it can replicate itself rapidly. But it doesn't need an executable life to infect the host node. It can enter a system by exploiting vulnerabilities in the network and then propagate from one node to another via file transfer mechanisms.

How to Combat Viruses and Worms?

In order to combat viruses and worms a number of measures need to be employed in tandem for best results.

1. The Operating System of the node needs to be updated frequently. This ensures that if strengthening of the OS to remove exploits has

been done by the vendor it is updated to all relevant nodes.

2. A good anti-virus is a must. It is capable of detecting and eliminating viruses and worms with efficiency and an updated malware base is a great way to protect against security issues.
3. A firewall should be in place and configured according to the safety needs of the network. This can prevent malicious code from entering the network in the first place.

What is Spyware?

A Spyware is a code snippet or a program which is aimed at:

1. Gathering information about the user covertly without his knowledge which can then be used for identity thefts or blackmailing.
2. Slowing down a computer or causing it to crash.
3. Opening several annoying pop-up windows and advertisements which mar user experience.

Spyware generally originates from mal coded sites and comes with downloads or software solutions. They can change the configuration of the computer or the browser without user knowledge and are difficult to remove. Since the adverse effects of spyware are less conspicuous or drastic than malware, they are not given due importance while setting up security measures.

How to Combat Spyware?

Spyware once installed is notoriously difficult to get rid of. In this case prevention is better than cure. Users should:

1. Always read instructions while installing new software carefully and decline all requests to change default search engines or browser additions.
2. Use anti-spyware solutions
3. Download software and other media ONLY from sites they trust which have the No Spyware or Malware certificate.

Difference Between Malware and Spyware?

MALWARE	SPYWARE
Malware is a broad term encompassing all the bits of maliciously coded software like viruses, worms, bots and Trojan Horses which are created with the sole purpose of entering the network, infecting the nodes and causing them to crash or malfunction	Spyware on the other hand is a more specific type of software designed to track and spy on the users.
Malware cause adverse effects that are drastic and immediate.	Spyware may in some cases keep track of relatively innocent information like browsing history or in extreme cases steal passwords and identities.
Malware can be detected and removed easily by a good anti-virus solution.	Spyware is difficult to spot. Sometimes the only side effect is a slight slowing down of the processing cycle of the CPU[111]. It can be

	eliminated with specialized anti-spyware solutions which are different from anti-viruses.

Hacking and Data Encryption

What is hacking?

Strictly speaking hacking refers to technical activities which are carried out experimentally to probe the capacity and functionality of a system. The malicious efforts by cyber criminals to cause harm to a system or to indulge in various kinds of thefts is called Cracking. However in layman's terms both hacking and cracking are considered synonymous and hacking is the term widely used to refer to malicious computer attacks and what we shall use here. Hacking/Cracking is the process by which **certain individuals (termed as computer hackers) utilize technically advanced software solutions in order to gain access to restricted portions of a network/node and manipulate the normal functioning of the node**. Hacking also involves appropriation of sensitive data and exploitation of vulnerabilities to render a system compromised.

What are the Different Types of Hacking?

The broad categorization of hacking is done on the basis of the intention behind the hacking.

1. **WHITE HAT HACKING** – White hat hacking or ethical hacking is the domain of security experts and testers. These individuals hack or break into

security systems with the explicit permission of an organization in order to test and expand the limitations of the security systems, firewalls and ciphers (keys used for encryption).

2. **BLACK HAT HACKING**- Black hat hacking is illegal and is not performed with the consent of an organization. Black hat hackers or crackers break into a system with ill intent and can cause data loss, financial loss and severe damage to a system.

3. **GREY HAT HACKING**- This is difficult to define. Grey hat hackers do not have malicious intent per se. But they do hack vulnerable sites without previous authorization. However they do so in order to bring the vulnerability to the notice of the organization and thus charge a sum of money to fix it.

4. **KIDDIE SCRIPT HACKING**- This type of hacking is carried out by amateurs using pre-written or automated hacking tools by people who are hackers themselves.

Hacking Societies

Hacking societies or forums are **platforms which allow hackers to congregate and develop new tools to revolutionize the world of hacking**. Most are white hat and actually work to fight the malicious codes and techniques structured by black hat hackers or crackers to harm victims. The most prominent hacking society by far is the group **Anonymous.**

It is a decentralized group of hackers who do not conduct themselves on any strictly defined policy. They generally launch hack attacks as a form of protest against government rules or policies. They seem to have a loosely agreed upon agenda which they then set about accomplishing. Starting with the 2008 **Project Chanology** which was aimed at the Church of Scientology, the

Anonymous hackers also called **"Anons"** became increasingly associated with international hacking campaigns to protest global occurrences/policies/changes in collaboration with other hacking societies.

What is Encryption?

Encryption is the process by which simple data or information is converted into code with the help of a key so that the resulting cipher text is not understood easily by hackers and eavesdroppers. The science of studying encryption-decryption methods is termed as Cryptography which in Greek means "Secret Writing". The main components of the process of encryption are:

1. The plaintext- The original unencrypted data or information
2. The cipher- This is the encryption-decryption algorithm
3. The key- This is a set of numbers upon which the cipher operates in order to produce the cipher text.
4. The cipher text- The ultimate encoded message which is sent to the receiver.

At the receiving end the cipher text is again decrypted using the cipher and the key in order to obtain the plaintext. There are three main types of encryption processes:

1. **Symmetric encryption**- In this type of encryption method the sender and receiver both use the same key termed as the "Secret" key. It is never made public and is in possession of ONLY the sender and the receiver. Symmetric key cryptography mostly uses traditional ciphers which are either **substitution based** or **transposition based.**
   • In substitution ciphers each character of the plaintext is substituted with another character. In some cases every time the

character say A occurs in the plaintext, it is always substituted with the letter C. This is called **Mono-substitution**. In some cases A can be substituted with different characters depending upon its position in the plaintext. This is termed as **Poly-substitution**. The substitution box or S Box is an example of this type of encryption.

- In **transposition** ciphers each character of the plaintext is not substituted. Instead the characters change position. Say the character in the first place goes to the eighth, the one in the eighth goes to the twelfth and so on. The P box or Permutation box is an example of this type of encryption.

2. **Asymmetric encryption-** In asymmetric encryption, there are two keys- the Public and the Private keys which together form a key pair. The Public key is, as the name suggests, public; it can be published on the internet as it does not have to be kept secure and both the sender and the receiver are in possession of it. The Private key belongs ONLY to the receiver. The sender encrypts the data with the Public key and this can only be decrypted by the private key. Should the receiver wish to send any information back securely they could then ask the other party to publish a public key so they can encrypt their return data with it, data that then could only be decrypted by the matching private key held only in possession of the other party. Rivest, Shamir, Adelman (RSA) is an example of asymmetric key cryptography. It is one of the most widely used methods to encrypt a small portion of a message like say a signature. It is extremely robust and it can take hackers so much processing power to break it down to make it unviable to even attempt it.

3. **Hashing-** The earliest and simplest form of

encryption, in hashing generally a small fixed length signature is created for the plaintext. Even a small change in the text can cause a drastic change in the hash and thus the receiver can suspect potential alteration with the data.

Examples of Encryption

With most online users becoming aware of the pitfalls of unsecured transactions and surfing, encryption is becoming increasingly widespread. It is used in:

1. **Authentication or digital signatures** where text is encrypted with a private key by the user and sent over to a number of recipients who possess the public key. Only they can decrypt, read and sign the document.
2. **Time Stamping** which is a unique procedure by which the exact time at which a document or data package was delivered or received can be verified and recorded. It uses the encryption method termed as Blind Signature Scheme[112] wherein a person can get a message signed by a party without revealing little or any information about the message content to the party.
3. **Online transactions and e-money transactions** wherein electronic funds are credit or debited to a particular account use Blind Signature Schemes. They must be doubly reinforced and protected from hacking attempts because money is directly involved.
4. **SSL (Secure Socket Layer) certificates** also use the RSA method of encryption. It provides secure data transfer between the layered network model and various application layer protocols like http and FTP.

Thus network security is a vast and multitudinous field

which is ever changing and ever evolving. It is in the best interest of individuals and organizations to invest in the right defences and educate themselves and their employees to ensure the integrity of their systems and their data.

Chapter 8

Voice over Internet Protocol (VOIP)

VOIP (Voice over Internet Protocol) is a method of taking analogue telephone signals and transmitting them over a digital network (such as the Internet). VOIP is being used today to make telephone calls over the Internet. It is in widespread use today, by individuals and businesses as well as telecommunications companies. Chances are, even if you do not have VOIP, when you make a long distance call it will at some point go over the Internet.

VOIP provides an interface to the PSTN (Public Switched Telephone Network), which is the technology used for analogue telephone calls that dates back over 100 years – the first telephone call is recognized as being placed in 1876. This interface to the PSTN network is what helps gives VOIP its versatility, since a VOIP phone can call an analogue phone.

VOIP is a mature technology, dating back to 1996. This is the year the first Internet phone software came to the market. Vonage, now a major provider, started in 2001. Skype, another major provider which is now owned by Microsoft, started in 2003. VOIP software, called a softphone and provided by companies such as Skype, allows two computer users, both running the VOIP phone software, to use their PCs to talk to each other. Over the years, VOIP has improved, and now it is possible to make calls using built in PC software, using an IP phone, or using an ATA (Analogue Telephone Adapter) with your analogue telephone. More on these terms later.

One of the first industries to make widespread use of VOIP technology was the call-centre industry. Call centres need to switch a huge amount of calls to a large number of phones. Analogue telephone switches were large, expensive and unwieldy. The call centre industry was quick to recognize the advantage of VOIP, since the data was in digital form and could easily be switched by routers and computers. A call centre network centre using VOIP can make widespread use of computers to switch calls.

Over the years, standards for VOIP have been introduced. SIP (Session Initiation Protocol) and H.323 are two of the most common protocols in use today. SIP was defined by the IETF (Internet Engineering Task Force). H.323 was defined by the ITU (International Telecommunications Union). Other protocols in use include MGCP (Media Gateway Control Protocol), H.248 (also known as Media Gateway Control Protocol) and RTP (Real-Time Transport Protocol). SIP and H.323 are the most common.

So how does VOIP work? VOIP works by converting the analogue signals of your voice into digital signals which can be transmitted over the Internet. A traditional type of VOIP installation uses an ATA (Analogue Telephone Adapter) to accomplish this task. The ATA plugs into your Internet router over an Ethernet type connection and the analogue telephone is plugged into the ATA. The ATA on the transmitting end incorporates a CODEC (Coder-Decoder) which samples the analogue telephone signal thousands of times per second and converts each small piece into digital data. In this instance the CODEC is acting as Coder. The ATA then handles the transmission of the digital data over the Internet by maintaining a session with the receiving end. The ATA on the receiving end then takes the digital data, and using a CODEC, converts the digital data back into analogue form and sends it to the analogue telephone. In this instance the CODEC is acting as a decoder.

We mentioned VOIP softphone clients earlier. This is software running on your PC that turns it into an IP telephone. Vonage was one of the first VOIP providers, and at the time they used a softphone exclusively. Skype, another large VOIP provider, also primarily uses this method today. A softphone uses the sound card on your PC to convert the analogue and digital signals. The interface usually looks like a telephone on your screen, with all the buttons you are used to seeing. With the addition of normally an external USB microphone/headset (but internal microphone and speakers can be used if available on your system) you can use the softphone to make calls over the Internet.

Another device used in VOIP installations is the IP phone. An IP phone is essentially an analogue telephone that looks just like your regular phone, but with a built-in ATA. The IP phone has an RJ-45 Ethernet or USB connector that allows you to plug it directly into your computer network.

Another type of VOIP phone is the VOIP Cell Phone. This is a phone that contains a regular cell phone that works over a radio frequency network as well as a built-in ATA and Wi-Fi connection. Whenever the cell phone is in reach of an accessible Wi-Fi connection, it will switch from the cell phone radio to VOIP for placing and receiving calls.

One advantage of VOIP is that it allows you to take your

phone with you when you travel. All you need is a broadband Internet connection to place phone calls. If you have a softphone, you can take your laptop along and plug it into an Internet connection. If you have an ATA, you can take it along and plug it into the Internet. You will also need to take your analogue telephone with this method. And if you have an IP phone, you can plug it directly into the Internet.

Another advantage of VOIP is that it can allow you to place calls over the Internet for free. Skype is a good example of this. You can download the Skype software and call other Skype users running the Skype software for free. Skype even offers video calls, which use technology known as Video over IP. Video over IP works similar to VOIP, but requires more bandwidth.

Bandwidth is a consideration with all of these VOIP and Video over IP methods. A dial-up connection does not have enough bandwidth to handle VOIP, so broadband Internet access is a necessity. A typical VOIP call requires about 90Kbps of bandwidth. This is not enough to place an appreciable load on the average broadband Internet connection. VOIP also requires a response time between endpoints of less than 150ms for optimal call quality. (See chapter 3 for details on how to measure this using the ping command). Video over IP requires more bandwidth, typically about 1-2M bps. This varies depending on the video quality. A low-resolution webcam can use less than 1 Mbit/s, while HD video can require 1-3 Mbit/s. For this reason, HD video usually uses a technique call interlacing, which cuts down on bandwidth requirements. In addition, HD video is usually compressed before being sent.

VOIP offers many calling features, and usually costs less than analogue telephone service. Most VOIP providers offer caller id with name, call waiting, call transfer, call block, repeat dial, return call and three-way calling.

Advanced features are available from some providers. These include call forwarding, anonymous call block, sending calls to voice mail, checking voice mail over the Internet and attaching voice messages to an email.

There are some disadvantages to VOIP. One is that the technology relies on the electric power grid for power. We have all experienced power outages, and we know that analogue telephones still work during a power outage. This is because the telephone company uses generators to back up the electricity needed for analogue phone calls. This is not the case with VOIP. With VOIP, if you are using a softphone, the PC does not have power to run the softphone application. Your internet connection is also likely dependent on a mains powered router. An ATA is the same, it plugs into the mains and will not have power during a power outage. The same is true with an IP phone, it uses mains power. If you have internet service from a cable provider, the ATA built into the router will not have power. This is not as big a disadvantage as it used to be as we now have widespread availability of mobile phones which can be used in such an emergency as they will continue to work during a power outage – providing the mobile phone is charged and that at least one of your local mobile base stations has power.

Another disadvantage of VOIP is calling the emergency services. Depending on where you live and what service provider you are using, the 911/999 operator may not be able to determine your geographic location when you place an emergency call. This is important because you may be disabled or unable to speak, and the emergency operator has no way of knowing where to dispatch the call. Again, this is not as big a disadvantage as it used to be. Most VOIP providers use a database to match your IP address with your physical location. This is made available to the emergency call centres. In the United States this is called E911 service. Standards have been implemented in this

114

area, and chances are nowadays if you have VOIP from a major provider, the emergency services operator has access to your geographic location.

Another disadvantage of VOIP is security. The VOIP industry has come a long way in this area, but security is still a concern. Hackers can hack into your connection and "eavesdrop" on your calls. In this way they may be able to obtain confidential information. This is not a huge concern nowadays as by default a lot of traffic now has basic encryption applied, but it is still a risk. If you were a head of state or a CEO discussing sensitive matters, a VOIP connection over the internet would not be an appropriate form of communication.

One other disadvantage of VOIP is that you are subject to the hiccups and outages that normally happen with your Internet connection. In other words you are bandwidth-dependent. If some other application or device on your network is using a lot of bandwidth, call quality can suffer. This can cause garbled calls, dropped calls and static. As the Internet becomes more reliable, this is also not as big a disadvantage as it used to be. In call centre and business applications VOIP uses a process called Call Monitoring to ensure quality. VOIP Call Monitoring uses hardware and software to test, analyse and rate the overall quality of VOIP calls in a VOIP network. Corrective action can be taken based on this quality analysis. Another disadvantage is that not all VOIP providers support faxing over the Internet. A fax signal is different than a voice signal, and some VOIP equipment does not have the necessary circuitry to accept the fax signal.

VOIP has advantages as well. One is cost. VOIP service, particularly long distance, is traditionally cheaper than analogue telephone service. Savings can be quite significant, and in some cases, such as with Skype mentioned earlier, you can place calls for free.

Another advantage is the wealth of features. Onco the analogue data is in digital form, it opens up a whole new range of features which can be implemented. We have already mentioned the Video over IP phone, which allows you to make face-to-face calls. Conference calls with multiple participants are easier to set up and implement with VOIP.

You can set up a conference call with multiple participants from your VOIP phone without the intervention of an operator. This can even be a video conference call with certain softphone software. We have already mentioned the capability of sending voice messages via e-mail. Another advantage is the ability to take your phone (and the associated cost savings) with you when you travel.

If you are using a softphone, VOIP provides another saving in the cost of the equipment required. If you already have the computer, all you have to add is a headset/microphone combination, which can be bought for less than the cost of an analogue telephone, a lot of laptops have a microphone and speakers built in, but call quality would be poorer compared to a dedicated device.

Another advantage of VOIP is local number portability. We have already mentioned that you can take your phone with you. An advantage of this is that your local phone number goes with the softphone or VOIP hardware. So no matter where you are in the world, your friends, family and business associates can still reach you by dialling your local number. This is called a virtual phone number, because it is not tied to one physical place.

A further advantage is integration and collaboration with other applications. VOIP protocols run on the application layer, meaning they can interact with other applications. We have already mentioned email, but VOIP can interact with many other applications, including web browsers (click to call), instant messenger and social networks, this creates many possibilities for integrating VOIP to existing applications and services.

Another advantage is the user control interface (usually a web GUI) offered by most VOIP providers. This allows you to easily make changes in your settings, for example setting up call forwarding or changing the number your phone is forwarded to.

In summary VOIP is a mature technology that has allowed the digital revolution to transform the telephone landscape, both in terms of how we place and make calls and also the underlying infrastructure that carries these calls. Its use is becoming more widespread at a rapid rate. Since VOIP data can be sent over a fibre optic cable with many other calls, the traditional analogue phone companies are using it more and more. If current trends continue all telephone traffic will one day be using VOIP services.

Chapter 9

Julian Assange, Edward Snowden and the Price we all Pay for our Connected World

It's a hazard of the information age. News travels fast, and disappears faster. Short, quick media pieces are money makers; sustained coverage is not. Little surprise that, according to Google Trends[113], interest in Edward Snowden lasted around one month, from June to July of 2013. Interest in Julian Assange[114] peaked in December of 2010, and hasn't reached comparable heights since.

At the time of writing today's media frenzy[115] is concerned about Miley Cyrus's questionable status as a sex goddess[116]. It treats Julian Assange and WikiLeaks (the organization famous for publishing proof of US government and corporate misconduct[117] in Iraq, Afghanistan, and Guantanamo Bay) as ancient history. Edward Snowden, and his shocking insights into the underbelly of US government surveillance, is going that way, too. Multibillion-dollar media conglomerates[118] have a vested interest in keeping it that way.

Assange and Snowden's relegation to mass media's proverbial back burner is not just about profit, it's about power. Why? They threaten the Information Technology (IT) structures that mass media depends on to survive. IT is the backbone of not only our political (including military) and economic systems, but also, and increasingly the medium by which we, the people, chose to conduct our private lives. Almost absolutely everything is run through a computer. Most of it is run through the internet. A government or a corporation's ability to control IT means that it can also monitor and control not only our economic choices, but also our belief systems and our private lives.

Not only this, control over IT dangerously redefines ideas of state sovereignty, mainly because the internet does not stop with the borders of any given country. A government or a corporation's control over the internet gives them the ability to manipulate populations of people far beyond their political borders. Therein lies the threats that Julian Assange and Edward Snowden pose: they have taken leaps towards forcing the Information Age out of the hands of media moguls, IT corporations and their government allies, and turning it over to the hands of 'we the people'.

Understanding the IT That's Making a Mockery of Law

Instead of other reporting that is intent on turning Snowden's and Assange's private life into soap-operas for mass-consumption, I will attempt to break down, and do homage to, what they're really trying to expose. This chapter examines and explains how governments and corporations are using IT as a weapon of mass control. It does so under the assumption that our understandings of them are key to standing up for our own civil and human rights.

Let's break things down: Assange and Snowden challenge the complete and utterly secret control of information by a powerful few. Control of this information starts with the systematic collection and mass-storage of all sorts of data from major internet and telecommunications providers like

AT&T, Verizon, Sprint, Facebook, Apple, Google, Microsoft, Yahoo, and AOL to name but a few.

Much of this is metadata[119], something used to describe the who, what, when of phone-calls, emails, text messages, etc. Other programs can be used to track the actual content of phone calls, emails, and financial transactions. Of course, as many other analyses have noted, metadata in itself is often more useful to governments than taking the time to read the content of messaging. It effectively tracks who goes where to talk to who and when. It knows, for example, if you went to the barber instead of going to church. It knows if you are friends with animal rights activists or Wall Street bankers. It is information that is so private that Slate Magazine compares it[120] to the DNA of your life.

The US government collects it on a global scale. Edward Snowden's leaks show that the most spied-on countries[121] by the United States Government are Iran, Pakistan, Jordan, Egypt, and India, in that order. (Purportedly, the U.S. government has a staggering 54.1 billion piece of information about the activities of people in those countries, alone.) In other words, the US is taking steps towards intruding and mapping (and thereby controlling) the intimate lives of the entire world.

How, exactly?

The USG and ally corporations collect this data using at least a couple of different techniques that we know about, largely thanks to the revelations of Edward Snowden.

One of these is the "upstream collection[122]" of data. The upstream collection of data means taking data directly from the 'main arteries[123]' that make up the internet: fibre-optic undersea telecommunication cables. These arteries are responsible for transporting over 99%[124] of the world's telecommunications. The USG does this either by way of their own taps, or by collaborating with foreign governments and foreign and domestic telecommunications companies.

Fibre Optic Splitters and Back Door Collections

As early as 2006-- well before the world knew about Snowden-- AT&T technician Mark Klein came forward to show us how this is done. Klein's evidence revealed that AT&T had installed a "fibre-optic splitter[125]," which automatically made and sent copies of all AT&T customers' emails and other internet activity to the USG's intelligence agency, the NSA. One such splitter used by the USG, Narus Semantic Traffic Analyzer[126], can analyze up to 10 gigabits of data a second.

While the NSA might go through the so-called proper processes (court orders, search warrants, etc.) to conduct some of this data collection, all signs point to most of it being conducted through the "back door[127]": in secret and behind the backs of even companies themselves. It is a project sometimes called "BULLRUN[128]," started in 2000[129], that works to decrypt just about anything on the internet.

BULLRUN seems to achieve this almost entirely through foul play. Sometimes, the NSA opts to deploy malware[130]. Malware depends on tricking a computer user into visiting a website under the NSA's control, and getting them to download a software that can then monitor everything that the computer does. A set of USG servers called "Quantum[131]" occupy the internet's arteries, and work to automatically direct people to webpages under the government's control. To gain access to the computer, once on the website, the website user can be tricked into downloading an infected software, or alternatively, the government can exploit the processes involved in loading and running a website (loading browser plugins and executing Java Script codes).

The NSA also breaks into private communications of the world's population by working hand in hand with software companies to infect the software that is supposed to provide private network protections[132]. Essentially, every time such software activates-- when people send emails, buy things online, or use 4G networks-- the NSA gains the key-code necessary to access the user's private information. According to Reuters[133], the NSA apparently paid the RSA (one of the biggest computer security providers) $10 million to break into their Bsafe software, which is used by most large technology companies and should "protect" the personal computers of millions of people.

The cliff notes are as follows: the USG pours millions of dollars a year into creating backdoors like this and ensuring that people "only have access to compromised systems[134]" and it's extremely effective. The Washington Post[135] reports that through upstream collection alone, every 14.4 seconds the U.S. government processes one Library of Congress worth of information, which makes for between 15-20 trillion transactions[136] over the past 11 years.

PRISM

The NSA does not always use the backdoor. Sometimes it knocks on the front door, using PRISM[137], which allows the government to streamline requests for information directly from U.S. telecommunications service-providers. PRISM collects not only metadata, but also the actual content[138] of emails, chats, VOIP[139] (Voice over IP) Calls, and cloud-stored[140] files. The NSA considers the program a complement to upstream data collection, which sometimes cannot easily crack encryption to access the actual content of files.

PRISM documents leaked by Edward Snowden show that the U.S. Government has direct access[141] to Microsoft, Yahoo, Google, Facebook and other companies. While the government can supposedly only collect data through PRISM with an official FISA Court[142] (Foreign Intelligence Surveillance Court, FISC) order, the FISC proceedings and rulings are completely secret. Furthermore, the Chief Judge of the FISA court admits[143] that the court depends completely on the information that the NSA provides to make its rulings. It has no authority or capability to monitor the NSA or stop NSA abuses. As such, it's hard to judge the scope or content of information retained through PRISM.

The Power of Information

The USG is putting unquantifiable resources into collecting and processing an unquantifiable amount of information. Why is this important?

Consider, first, that the government cannot and should not be viewed as in any way independent from giant media moguls and IT corporations. The State Department and Silicon Valley are brothers. Not only do they work closely together to achieve economic and political objectives, but they are also incestuous. Prime Example: Jared Cohen, who moved from being adviser to Condoleezza Rice and Hillary Clinton to director of Google Ideas[144]. The NSA, on the other hand, pays over 1,000 private contractors[145] to do its work.

Simply put, one can no longer be clear where corporation ends and government begins. And when you know everything, you not only control everything, but you also limit what everybody else knows and controls. The potential reach of this is enormous. Money transactions in the world are routed through the United States. In a stock-based economy, entirely reliant on electronic infrastructure, foreknowledge of company decision making plans, and monitoring the economic preferences of millions of people has enormous profit-generating potential.

It's more than just about economics. When you control money flow, you control the decisions of not only corporations, but also millions and millions of people. When WikiLeaks broke, the United States showed the extent of this control by asking PayPal and Amazon to freeze the organization's funds[146]. In total, WikiLeaks found over 100,000 euros worth of funds frozen overnight, putting the entire operation into serious jeopardy.

Imagine, too, the propaganda and political-messaging potentials when social networks like Gmail, Facebook, and Twitter give you insight into everybody's private lives and thought processes. Julian Assange's book *Cyberpunks: Freedom and the Future of the Internet*[147] compares information sharing on Facebook to the East German Security State. Where people were paid off in East Germany for being part of its police and surveillance agency, the Stasi, they are compensated with social credits-- like "get[ing] laid by their neighbour"-- for participating in Facebook.

What results is a system of social and ideological control, jealously guarded by censorship. Communication companies and media moguls, working closely with the government, publish what suits their, and the government's, political and economic objectives. What gets published and what doesn't get published is entirely up to them. Without the approval, backing or leveraging of the large corporations that guide the average internet user through the maze, publishing anything on the internet is unlikely to find a mass audience.

It's next to impossible to defeat this censorship. When WikiLeaks went under fire, payment providers, service providers and visualization software services cut off their services[148]. The organization only survived because thousands of copycat sights reproduced its information. Then, as *Cyberpunks*[149] documents, all U.S. Government agencies blocked access of WikiLeaks through their networks, and academic Institutions were warned to tell their students that if they were considering careers in public services, not to use WikiLeaks in research or otherwise.

When reinforced by the control over economics, a system of censorship like this is usually powerful enough to stop journalists from publishing any potentially controversial materials, simply because they could never make a living doing it. Should all else fail, it's a system that also ensures that should huge media outlets publish anything 'politically unsavory,' not only the article, but the record of the article is likely to be wiped clean from the internet as if it had never existed. For example, *CyberPunks* documents how *The New York Times* erased an article claiming that the US had used oil companies in Libya to distribute bribes to local politicians.

In an age where a few powerful corporations and governments ingest everybody's private life, controlling and defining information access literally molds the reality we live in. It is a constructed reality that seems more often than not to be used to wage war and otherwise wreak havoc. The US military calls IT a "force multiplier": controlling the precision of weapons, determining the when's and where's of strikes, and misleading and manipulating opposition forces. It's the key component in a U.S. run, and increasingly violent, global security state, with a growing totalitarian presence.

The Threat Assange Poses

How can Assange possibly pose a threat to this? Through WikiLeaks[150], Assange and his co-workers have published over 1.2million[151] documents provided by anonymous sources and protected through website encryption that ensures nobody can trace its source. Simply put, the existence of the website threatens the U.S. government's monopolization, and thus control and manipulation of, information. In doing so, WikiLeaks gives people the power to form their own opinions and participate in democratic processes unavailable to them in a world where only censored versions of information are available.

Damages thereby inflicted on the U.S. Security State are real, and building. WikiLeaks is undermining the U.S.'s top money maker, the production of war:

In 2010, the website proved US connections to drone strikes in Yemen[152] and the secret deal the US government made with Yemen's president to allow the strikes. The website may also be responsible for bringing US troops home from Iraq[153]. CNN reports that negotiations to keep US military presence in Iraq fell apart after WikiLeaks published a document showing that the U.S. covered up the fact that US soldiers knowingly killed innocent women and children.

Its influence is spreading, and with it, it's potential danger to the US's political and economic objectives. Trends show that mainstream news sources have begun to rely on WikiLeaks documents. Atlantic Wire reports[154] that in 2011, half of *New York Times*[155] reports relied on the source.

The Threat Snowden Poses

Snowden's revelations undermine the system from a slightly different angle. Instead of providing alternative information sources as Assange did, Snowden exposed the system itself, a system contingent on secrecy.

Consider that mass surveillance is not compatible with the supposedly democratic governments that conduct it. It depends on secret courts, secret court decisions, and almost no oversight from any branch of government. Most data lifted through upstream data collection and through PRISM are only subject to the supervision of what's called a FISA court (FISC). A company that receives a FISC order to release information to the NSA is prohibited from even talking about the fact that it's received one[156]. The FISC itself has no oversight power over the NSA, and relies solely on the information the NSA gives it.

If the FISC has no oversight power, all reports released to date[157] show that neither do the executive branch nor congress, members of which either know very little about NSA operations or are prohibited from talking about what they do know.

There is simply no way to ingest mass amounts of information without abusing people's privacy rights: abuse is built into the system. One report released[158] shows that between April of 2011 and March of 2012, the NSA violated the privacy of U.S. citizens over 2,776 times and I would expect the true figure to be significantly higher. There is no accurate reporting on how many times it's violated the rights of global citizens.

Just by making a secret system more public, Snowden did his damage. But his contributions go beyond that. His revelations have started a discussion about the powers of IT that have taken huge strides towards making the inner workings of the communications and internet world accessible to the people. Suffice to say that, thanks to Snowden, we are gaining the tools to break down this Security State on two levels: on a personal level, by proactively using the communications and internet in ways that protect ourselves from infringements on our privacy, and also on a political level, to pressure for true, democratic policy changes.

In a world whose economic and political systems are increasingly governed by the structures of IT, Assange and

Snowden must be viewed as more than whistleblowers. They challenge the ability of the US Government and its allies to control economics, ideology, and wage war. This is guerrilla warfare, on a global level.

What About Snowden and Assange Make Them Successful?

It's worth taking a moment to consider why these two men were able to make such a big impact. Who are these new Guerrilla warriors? Why wasn't the greatest security apparatus in the world able to completely censor them?

Consider their identities. Neither Snowden nor Assange are Muslim. They are not Middle Eastern or Asian looking. They are not undocumented immigrants. They do not even come from poor families. They are not violent. They have all the privileges associated with not-unattractive, white, middle class, educated men.

According to *Time* Magazine[159], Assange was born in 1971 in Townsville, northeastern Australia. He was homeschooled, and eventually went on to study math and physics at the University of Melbourne. In 1991, he plead guilty to breaking into the master terminal of Nortel, a Canadian telecom company. Miraculously, his only punishment was a small fine. (In his ruling, the judge purportedly cited Assange's "intelligent inquisitiveness.") Assange dropped out of the University of Melbourne when he found that the university's work was being used by defense contractors and militaries. In 2006, he founded WikiLeaks.

Snowden's story is similar. *The Guardian*[160] reports that Snowden grew up in Elizabeth City, North Carolina. He studied computing at a community college in Maryland, where he would eventually drop out. Later, he received his GED. In 2003, Snowden enlisted in the U.S. Army, which opened the door for him to work for the NSA. By 2007, he was working for the CIA in Geneva Switzerland. By 2012, Snowden was living in Hawaii, making $200,000 a year as an employee for the defense contractor Booz Allen Hamilton, which subcontracts to the NSA.

Censoring Assange and Snowden completely would be impossible, simply because both Snowden and Assange's identities perfectly mirror the image that the media empires and the U.S. government promotes as perfect citizens. It's hard to marginalize an image that you've spent hundreds of years building up.

Which is not to say that the USG has not tried. Mainstream media coverage ran extensive smear campaigns on both Snowden and Assange, trying to construe them as both political traders and sexually perverse people. In 2010, sexual assault charges[161] were brought against Assange in Sweden. Assange claims[162] that they are false, and meant only to attack his reputation. False or not, they have monopolized a good portion of Assange's news coverage. And, as a Guardian Commentary[163] rightly points out, both Swedish and British courts have mishandled the women's allegations by allowing them to become subject to a media frenzy. This breaks not only the rape victims' right to anonymity, but also the defendant's right to presumed innocence until proven guilty.

The U.S. government has also gone to great lengths to label Assange as an enemy and spy, indicting[164] WikiLeaks and Assange under the Espionage Act. (If convicted, WikiLeaks would be the first media organization to be convicted under the act. Many warn, that this could set the precedent for potentially being able to indict more journalists simply for, what former New York Times general counsel, James Goodale, calls[165] the "conspiracy to commit journalism.")

In Snowden's case, too, a major media smear campaign[166],

was more apt to criticize his sex life[167] than focus on the documents he leaked. Like Assange, the U.S. Government is intent on indicting Snowden and convicting him of treason. And in part, the campaigns worked. Both Snowden and Assange are virtually imprisoned. Assange is unable to leave the Ecuadorian Embassy in London, England, where he has been granted asylum. Snowden has been given temporary asylum and is trapped in Russia.

But in a big way, they have failed. Neither of Snowden nor Assange have sustained bodily harm. Neither of their messages have been silenced. A poll[168] commissioned by the Washington Post and ABC News last November showed that despite the best efforts of U.S. media, young adults under the age of 30 overwhelmingly support Snowden. Support for Assange remains strong, too, and a new WikiLeaks political party in Australia has garnered a surprising amount of support[169].

What's Changed in the IT World, and Where Do We Go from Here?

Despite the US government and the mass media's best attempts to minimize their damages, Assange and Snowden are changing the IT world. Both of their revelations have awakened the desire and harkened the need for a much more private, much more decentralized, and much more usable internet and communications-based IT geography.

It is a desire that is increasingly expressed en-masse through market choices; it is one that big US telecommunications corporations are finding it hard to ignore. Over the next three years, in the aftermath of Snowden, it is estimated[170] that the US tech industry will lose between $35 billion and $180 billion dollars. The examples of economic fallout are piling up. AT&T may not be successful[171] in its quest to buy European company Vodafone. Cisco has taken a hit, too. In November of last year, they reported[172] that Snowden's revelations cost them a 12% drop in their overall sales, losses most heavily felt in Brazil and Russia. And then there are the reports[173] that numerous foreign companies have started to cancel their cloud storage and computing contracts with US companies to try to avoid NSA snooping. One confirmed example[174] is Telenor, Norway's largest Telecom provider.

The market for internet privacy is driving real, proactive changes. On the one hand, major US companies-- including Microsoft, Google, Yahoo and LinkedIn-- have now (at least on face value) turned against the US government[175]. They are pressuring it to declassify documents that show how many times the companies have been asked to turn over information to the government and in what contexts.

But changes go beyond calls for transparency. In September of 2013, the National Institute of Standards and Technology warned companies against[176] using technologies that could be undermined by BULLRUN. Companies are responding by promising to use encryptions to make their services harder to wire-tap and more privacy oriented. Microsoft recently announced plans[177] to encrypt all of its data by default (instead of making it a personally-activated option). Google[178] and Yahoo[179] have similar plans.

Consider, too, the contributions of hundreds of smaller IT companies and organizations that have been gaining popularity since Assange. These are doing their best to provide not only private communication alternatives, but also the information needed so that users can proactively protect themselves. Mailpile[180] is an example. It's an open source, web-based email provider that and you can run it from your own computer or from the cloud, like google. As secure email sources like Mailpile gain popularity (and less secure email sources like Google lose clients), it will get harder and harder for the NSA to snoop for the simple reason that it's more expensive to subpoena hundreds of email providers.

Whistle blowing websites[181] similar to WikiLeaks, with heavily encrypted information sources, are also on the rise. OpenLeaks, LocalLeaks, Rospil, RuLeaks and GreenLeaks are all examples of websites that do similar work. Media mogul Aljazeera has also created a Transparency Unit, which is way to securely upload documents, photos, audio, videos and story tips. Rumors has it that the New York Times has a similar projects in the works.

Pressure from International Governing Bodies

Pressure does not stop in the form market-based demands. The United States, and US IT companies are taking the heat from international governing bodies. Numerous reports document how US American companies are increasingly forced to deal with unusual amounts of regulatory pressure and scrutiny[182] in the EU, China and South America.

It's an international pressure-push to decentralize the geopolitical governance of IT communications, that Brazil and Germany have taken the lead in. An alliance of German phone and Internet Companies are pushing[183] the German government to guarantee German phone and internet communications should only be transmitted within German borders. While this would not provide security for Germans surfing on foreign webpages (such as Facebook) it would supposedly increase security for internal communications by preventing them from bouncing outside the country.

Brazil's government has gone a step further. In the wake of Snowden's revelations, the Brazilian government canceled a military contract[184] with the US for Boeing F/A-18 fighter jets and has elected to instead buy its jets from Sweden. Similar to Germany, the Brazilian government is also considering the passage of a law that would require US companies to store data about Brazilian customers inside Brazil[185], instead of offshore. According to Google itself[186], should this, and similar laws be passed, companies like Google might be prevented from doing business in some of the world's biggest markets. In reality it would mean that they have to invest in regional data centres which would come at a financial cost to these companies.

On a regional level, European Union leaders have purportedly banded together[187] to advocate the creation of cloud-data storage independent from the United States. The pending US-EU free trade agreement is acting as a pressure point[188] to press this issue. The African Union, for its part, is also working to establish a common cybersecurity framework[189], covering national cybersecurity, electronic commerce and cybercrimes.

And, on a global level, in December of last year, Brazil and Germany led the United Nations in the passage of a landmark resolution[190], "the right to privacy in the digital age." The resolution affirms that people's rights online, including the human right to privacy, must be the same as people's rights offline. It also affirms that these human rights are universal and cannot be broken simply because they live beyond the national borders of the country conducting the spying.

In short, Snowden and Assange have called into question the socio-political geography of IT that the US government relies on to push its political and economic objects. The decentralized, more democratic control over the IT world that they promote—and seem to be instigating through their actions—is in a lot of ways as threatening to the United States government and corporations as the spread of communist ideology during the Cold War.

The highly centralized, and abuse-ready structures of the internet have in no ways collapsed, and neither has the US government's ability to extract extremely private information from them. Both are, for the first time, under scrutiny and pressure. Individuals wishing to apply directly what pressure they are able to can do this by using more secure internet and telecommunication software, by continuing to educate themselves using sources of information other than that provided by the media conglomerates or the state and continuing discussions like this one.

Chapter 10

Biographies of Pioneers in the History of Networking

1. Leonard Bosack and Sandy Lerner, co-founders of Cisco

Leonard Bosack and Sandy Lerner are two pioneers of internet technology, developing internet routers from their Stanford University quarters. Born in 1952 in Pennsylvania, Leonard Bosack was a student of computer science. Sandy Lerner, born in 1955, was a political science major who went on to study computer science.

The year was 1984 and Leonard and Sandy were in love. Though, computer technology was just beginning to take wider root in the modern world, Leonard Bosack and Sandy Lerner are said to have wanted to create a way to send love letters from their separate buildings across campus to each other. To accomplish this specific aim, so the story goes, they joined forces in inventing a new, high tech way to allow communication between their own incompatible disconnected computers. Unfortunately this story does not have a solid basis in fact and is said to have been perpetuated by the Cisco company to hide the fact that the first equipment sold by the company was actually created by a team of individuals working at Stanford University, a fact that led to a lawsuit and a settlement in favour of the University.

What is beyond dispute is that Bosack and Lerner did create a new company named Cisco in 1984. Today, we know Cisco as the leading global corporation for electronic and technology services with a revenue of $48 billion in 2013. At one point during the infamous stock market tech bubble Cisco was, by market capitalization, the biggest company in the world. Their market capitalization has since been overtaken by other companies but in terms of sales and market demand for their products and services the company continues to grow. But how did the company really begin?

Leonard Bosack and Sandy Lerner met at Stanford University in 1979. They were both studying computer science. Not too long after they had met, they began dating and then married in 1980.

They had been experimenting at Stanford University in attempt to connect detached networks from the Computer Science lab building to the Business School lab building. They realized that in order to make the two different networks communicate with one another that they needed to have a technology that could connect the different local systems that were using different protocols. Working together and with colleagues at the University they created the multi-protocol router.

Upon the creation of the multi-protocol router, Leonard and Sandy made a proposal to Stanford University to build and sell routers, but in potentially one of the most flawed business decisions in history the University refused. Stanford's refusal actually opened the doorway to a revolutionizing decision that would forever change the market of commercialized internet technology. Leonard Bosack and Sandy Lerner decided to begin their own company. Thus, Cisco was born in 1984.

Cisco's name was derived from name of the nearby city of 'San Francisco'. At first, Leonard and Sandy were creating, designing and making the routers in their garage and living room of their home.

In parallel to the early years of Cisco in 1986 the 'Internet Engineering Task Force' (IETF) was formed. The Internet Engineering Task Force is known as an international community of the technological world that addresses concerns with the evolution and operation of intrinsic internet architecture. The IETF produces a set of vendor neutral standards to ensure that systems produced by different manufactures are compatible. It is thanks to these types of global networking standards produced by the IETF and other such organizations that we have a single internet and not several different incompatible global networks. It was these standards that Cisco would largely adhere to with their products and services.

In that same year, 1986, the company started selling their multi-protocol server, AGS (Advanced Gateway Server). This was merely a revised version of the Stanford router. In the first month of Cisco's sales they managed to land contracts that totaled over $200,000. This was an incredible feat for Cisco during their first month of sales and encouraged the couple to continue in their business endeavors. Leonard and Sandy's marketing strategies of commercializing their products allowed their company to grow exponentially.

By 1989, Cisco had 111 employees listed on payroll and were distributing three products to the world. Despite a small number of products and a limited staff, Cisco managed to deliver impressive sales figures. In 1989, their revenues soared to $27 million US. With each passing year, the company continued to grow rapidly.

Entering into the nineties, the growth of the internet was reaching a tipping point that was starting to change the world. On February 16, 1990, Cisco went public. They were listed as 'CSCO' on the NASDAQ and they also launched its Networkers Users Symposiums. Unfortunately, in that same year, the professional management team of Cisco fired Sandy Lerner. Leonard, in support of his wife, also walked away from Cisco. Even though these events were a disappointment to them both, they did not leave empty handed, walking away with around $170 million.

Even though Cisco lost its founding parents, the company continued to grow. In 1991, they began opening offices abroad in places such as Uxbridge near London in the UK and Courtabeouf in France. By 1996, the company achieved revenues of $5.4 billion. In just two more years, Cisco controlled over three-fourths of the world's router business, with offices in multiple cities worldwide. It also became the first company in history to reach a market capitalization of $100 billion in just fourteen years.

Today, the world knows Cisco as the global leader in routing, switching and network communications and a leading company in many other areas such as security. Cisco also focus on advanced technologies such as wireless LAN, home networks, IP communications, storage area networking and voice and video over IP. Any modern consumer using the internet will have, at some stage, their traffic running through Cisco products.

Technology is always changing, and Cisco recognizes that in order to maintain their market share they must continue to innovate. They continue to constantly invent, design and create new technologies that allows companies, organizations and even families easier, faster and more secure methods of communication and networking.

Although Leonard and Sandy divorced, they still participate together in a charitable foundation that has been trust funded with 70% of the money from the sale of their Cisco stock. Their charity is primarily involved with animal welfare and scientific projects. Amongst some of its interests it finances The Center for Conservation Biology at the University of Washington. Their foundation also purchased Chawton House, which is a manor house in England. It was once owned by the brother of renowned author, Jane Austen. Chawton House now serves as a research facility for the study of female writing. This personal connection with Jane Austen was evident as Sandy Lerner published a book, under a pseudonym, titled *Second Impressions* in November 2011 which was a sequel to Jane Austen's[191] *Pride and Prejudice*[192].

It is interesting to speculate how different networking, the internet and indeed the world be today had Leonard and Sandy not founded Cisco and started selling the multi-protocol router. Cisco became the backbone of the modern internet and their effective monopoly on networking technology in the early years of Cisco's growth allowed for global standards to be adopted and become widespread. Cisco is a corporation that has played a significant part in shaping our modern connected world.

2. Gordon Moore, founder of Intel and famous for Moore's Law

Early Years
Gordon Earle Moore was born on January 3, 1929 in San Francisco, California near his small farm community

hometown, Pescadero. Gordon Moore grew up enjoying fishing and hunting, with his mother, a homemaker and his father, who was a local law enforcement officer. Pescadero was moderately advanced for the time in a technological sense with basic innovations such as televisions and telephones.

Gordon Moore's interest in chemistry was sparked when a neighbour of his received a chemistry set. He soon developed an affinity to chemistry and its associated fields, mathematics and physics. Though Moore's mother had finished high school, his father had left school in seventh grade to support his family after the death of his father. With no real history of college attendance in his family, Moore's decision and ability to further his education was to lead to a significant change in his fortunes.

Gordon Moore first transitioned from high school to San Jose State University for his freshman and sophomore years of college, where he met his future bride, Betty. Influenced by his cousin's college roots in California's universities, Moore decided to transfer to the University of California, Berkley where he received his undergraduate degree in Chemistry in 1950.

Gordon Moore went on to pursue his graduate education at the California Institute of Technology, with a major in Chemistry and a minor in Physics, receiving his Ph.D. in 1954. After exploring various career options, Moore went to Johns Hopkins University for his Postdoctoral Research in the Applied Physics Laboratory, conducting research in missile development for the United States Navy. Moore completed his Postdoctoral Research in 1956.

With the counsel of his thesis advisor, Gordon Moore explored industrial opportunities upon completion of his formal education. Moore found employment at Shockley's Semiconductor Laboratory working for William Shockley.

William Shockley was a charismatic recruiter and had high hopes for the lab. He had assembled a top notch team, including Moore, even though Moore, at the time, didn't even know what a semiconductor was.

The small staff at Shockley's Semiconductor Laboratory grew close as they worked long hours together and sometimes under challenging circumstances.

The team discovered the results of psychological tests that Moore and others had been asked to take during the interview process, which stated that Moore and his colleague, Robert Noyce, would never be managers. Moore realized that this meant his time and options were limited. Due to Shockley's inconsistent managerial oversight, many of Shockley's employees were frustrated. One example was when Shockley put the entire staff through lie detector tests to determine who was to blame for a minor incident.

After searching for financial support, a team of Shockley's employees banded together and left the company, forming the Fairchild Semiconductor Corporation, backed by Sherman Fairchild.

The company's focus was to create silicon transistors, at a time when germanium was the primary material used for transistors. Silicon was coveted for its fine sand like quality and cheaper price point. This was a project that Shockley had abandoned in early production. The group learned from their mistakes at Shockley's and built a successful semiconductor company. The first transistor, 2N697, was a huge success with the group selling 100 transistors to IBM (International Business Machines). Fairchild's first resistors sold for $150 per piece but later models sold for a few dollars each.

In 1965, the Electronics Magazine requested an article

from Gordon Moore predicting the future of semiconductors and electronics. Gordon became known for this published paper, where he predicted that the number of transistors that would fit onto an integrated circuit, or a microchip, would increase by a factor of two every two years. Based on his years of experience with the technology, Gordon Moore was saying that computer technology would be capable of processing information twice as fast as before every two years. This principle became what was known as Moore's Law. Members of the computer science industry embraced this principle and in a lot of ways it became a self-fulfilling prophecy as competing manufacturers invested heavily in research and development to ensure their products kept pace with Moore's Law as they correctly assumed this was the benchmark their competitors were also working to. Moore's Law set the pace and the standard of progress for digital electronic devices, affecting processing speed, memory space, sensors and other measurements of technological productivity.

In the face of competition from Texas Instrument and other new start-ups, Robert Noyce and Gordon Moore secretly made plans to launch their own new company.

In 1968, Gordon Moore and Robert Noyce went on to co-found NM Electronics, which would later be renamed Intel Corporation. Moore served various leadership roles at the Intel Corporation from Executive Vice President to Board Chairman to the President. In 1997 he was named Chairman Emeritus of Intel.

Intel Corporation
Driven by Moore's Law, the Intel Corporation was focused on fast-paced innovation and was able to adhere to Moore's law doubling the speed, memory and performance of its microchips, for decades. Intel Corporation evolved into the world's largest semiconductor manufacturer.

Based in Santa Clara, California, Intel specialized in making devices related to computer and communication technology. Faced with competition from Japanese semiconductor manufacturers, Intel created the world's first microprocessor chip in 1971. With the launch of the personal computer, Intel quickly adjusted its focus to the personal computer industry.

Intel Corporation strategically positioned itself as the primary supplier of the microprocessor for personal computers. It has continued to innovate and decades later is still the world's leading chip maker with a revenue in 2012 of $53.34 billion US.

Community Roles
As a strong advocate of science education, Gordon Moore served as a member of the Gilead Sciences Advisory Board, before becoming part of the Board of Directors in 1996.

In 1983, Gordon Moore became a member of the trustee board of Caltech, or the California Institute of Technology. He became the chair of the board from 1993 to 2000 and now serves as a life trustee.

Gordon Moore and his wife, Betty Moore established a charitable foundation, donating $600 million to Caltech in 2001, with an aim of keeping the university at the forefront of innovation in technology. This was at the time the largest donation ever made to an educational institution. In 2007, Moore contributed an additional $200 million for the construction of the world's largest optical telescope, the Thirty Meter Telescope.

Gordon Moore's business sense, industry savvy and foresight ensured that his life and work had one of the most significant impacts on the history of computing.

3. Mark Zuckerberg, co-founder of Facebook

Overview

Worth an estimated $20 billion dollars, Mark Zuckerberg's Facebook empire has crowned him the king of social media. Named one of *Time* Magazine's 100 Wealthiest and Most Influential People, Mark Zuckerberg has been innovating in the field of technology from his youth.

Early Years

Born in White Plains, New York, Mark Zuckerberg was raised as a Jew by a psychiatrist (his mother) and a dentist (his father) in Dobbs Ferry, New York with three sisters. As a middle school student, Zuckerberg's father encouraged him in the field of computer sciences, teaching Mark the *Atari BASIC* program and even hiring a software developer to tutor him.

Zuckerberg excelled in information technology and soon developed a program he coined, "Zucknet", which would be comparable to Facebook's Instant Messenger of today. At the time this was a ground breaking use of technology. With this software, he was able to communicate with other computers within his household, sending his family members messages.

In high school, Mark Zuckerberg took a graduate course in computer programming from Mercy College. He went on to develop a program called Synapse, which anticipated users' listening preferences. Despite several offers from Microsoft and AOL, Zuckerberg refused to sell Synapse, even for millions of dollars.

Though information technology moguls attempted to recruit Zuckerberg out of high school, he chose instead to attend Harvard University.

Harvard

At Harvard University, Mark Zuckerberg further his reputation as a software genius. He developed a program, called CourseMatch, which helped students identify and schedule their classes with friends. This program also allowed students to develop study groups together, based on their course schedules.

Later, he went on to develop a program in which students could compare their peers according to their looks in a sort of "hot or not" game, called FaceMash. FaceMash was soon shut down by the university, being deemed inappropriate and for the unauthorized use of student's photos.

In January 2004, Mark Zuckerberg developed "The Facebook". In his sophomore year at Harvard University, Mark Zuckerberg left school to pursue Facebook full time.

The Emergence of Facebook

TheFacebook.com launched on February 4, 2004. Shortly after its launch, three of Mark Zuckerberg's colleagues at Harvard, Cameron Winklevoss, Tyler Winklevoss and Divya Nevendra, accused him of stealing the idea from them. During the development of the Facebook, the group had hired Mark to develop a website called, the *HarvardConnection.com.* They alleged that Mark Zuckerberg stole their ideas while building Facebook. During the time period when Zuckerberg was supposedly working on HarvardConnection.com, they alleged that he was using their ideas to develop a competing project, Facebook.

The group sued Zuckerberg, pledging to take the lawsuit to the Supreme Court, if necessary. Zuckerberg and the Winklevosses soon settled out of court for the equivalent of 1.2 million shares which was $300 million dollars.

The concept of Facebook was to allow people around the world to connect with one another by sharing updates, their likes, their photos and comments.

Facebook began at Harvard University and then expanded to MIT, Boston University, Boston College, Northeastern University, Stanford University, Dartmouth University, Columbia University and Yale University.

In June 2004, Zuckerberg received his first company investment from Peter Thiel who invested $500,000 dollars for an 11 percent share in the company. The same year, theFacebook.com incorporated with Sean Parker as its president, now based in Palo Alto, California. By December 2004, Facebook reached its one millionth user.

In early 2005, Facebook went international. In spite of its success, Facebook still suffered a net loss of $3.63 million for the Fiscal Year. Soon after, rumors spread that Facebook would be sold, after the acquisition of Myspace by business giants, News Corp. In September 2006, Yahoo offered to buy Facebook for $1 billion. However, Mark Zuckerberg refused. He set out to keep the majority of control over the company while, at the same time, attracting enough investors to fund the company's growth. Despite offers to sell the company, Zuckerberg maintains that his goal is not simply to make money, but to create an open environment for people to share with one another. This environment, in Zuckerberg's view, should not be controlled by these mega media corporations.

Facebook spread to high schools and then, the general public in September 2006. In September 2009, Facebook turned cash flow to positive for the first time. The company rapidly grew, adding popular features such as Community Pages, Instant Messenger, Friend Feeds and more.

Facebook continually grew by partnering with major companies like Yelp, Pandora and Skype to instantly populate a person's information into the application by signing in with Facebook.

In January 2011, $500 million were invested into Facebook, sending Facebook's worth sailing to $50 billion making Mark Zuckerberg the world's second youngest billionaire as of 2012.

Mark Zuckerberg's Vision

Mark Zuckerberg has been often advised by computer science magnates like Bill Gates and Steve Jobs. His international influence consistently rises. Zuckerberg has connected with international leaders, such as President Barack Obama and Russia's Prime Minister, Dmitry Medvedev.

In 2005, Mark Zuckerberg was named one of the top 35 innovators in the world under the age of 35 by MIT Technology Review TR35.

With over a billion Facebook users, Zuckerberg is working towards a goal of registering 5 billion Facebook users, most of which have yet to receive access to the internet. By providing internet to these offline people it is hoped that jobs will be created and new technology will provide growth and opportunities for some of the world's most underdeveloped regions.

Newark – Social Network Movie

In October 2010, *The Social Network* movie was released, later winning a Golden Globe Award for Best Picture. Though it was based on the development of Facebook and Mark Zuckerberg's life, it did not wholly portray Zuckerberg in a positive light, highlighting the controversy between Zuckerberg, the Winklevoss brothers and Divya Nevendra that eventually led to one of many lawsuits.

Mark Zuckerberg allegedly even considered making his planned contribution to the Newark, New Jersey Public Schools of $100 million an anonymous gift, in fear that the negative publicity would overshadow the impact of his philanthropy or be considered a crass publicity stunt. After coaxing from Newark Mayor, Corey Booker, Zuckerberg agreed to donate publicly.

His charitable contributions, including a $500 million gift to the Silicon Valley Community Foundation, are numerable. On December 19, 2013, Mark Zuckerberg pledged, with Bill Gates and Warren Buffet, to donate half of his wealth to charity over time.

As of 2014 Facebook has touched the lives of over a billion people but the story of Mark Zuckerberg and Facebook still has a lot of new chapters yet to be written.

4. Hewlett and Packard, co-founders of HP

Overview

Two pioneers of the technology industry, who reinvented the way the world thinks about electronic tools and instruments, are Dave Packard and William "Bill" Redington Hewlett. Hewlett and Packard began their company with a passion for precision and accuracy in all of their instruments and have evolved into an international business providing software, hardware and services on a global basis. The company serves individuals, small businesses, large enterprises, educational sectors and governments with their products and services.

They initially met at Stanford University, and developed a lifelong friendship and partnership that would impact millions of lives throughout the world. When founding the company the duo decided to use their surnames as the company name and it was a toss of the coin that led to the company being called HP, had the coin flip turned out differently you would now be reading about the PH Company.

Starting out in a one car garage, Hewlett and Packard sold their first product, an audio processor. One of their first customers was Walt Disney who purchased eight for use in his movie, Fantasia. This processor helped provide the surround sound experience for the renowned film.

The company has come a long way since its origins; in 2007 it became the leading manufacturer of Personal Computers in the world, a feat it still holds as of 2014.

The Early Years of William "Bill" Redington Hewlett
Bill Hewlett was born in Ann Arbor, Michigan on May 20, 1913. Hewlett moved with his family to Stanford California, when his father moved his teaching position from the University of Michigan Medical School to Stanford University Medical School. Bill Hewlett's father died while he was attending Lowell High School. He was encouraged to attend Stanford University in remembrance of his father's legacy.

Bill excelled at Stanford University, graduating with a Bachelor's degree, and decided to continue at MIT to pursue a Master of Science Degree in electrical engineering. He later returned to Stanford and received the degree of Electrical Engineer in 1939. It was at Stanford University that Hewlett met Dave Packard.

The Early Years of Dave Packard
The other half of the team, Dave Packard was born on September 7, 1912 in Pueblo, Colorado. Dave showed a passion for engineering and science in his early years. He went on to attend Stanford University to pursue a degree in

electrical engineering.

Not only did Dave meet his business partner, Bill Hewlett, at Stanford University, but he also met his wife, Lucile Salter. After completing his undergraduate degree at Stanford, Dave Packard went to the University of Colorado for a short period of time. Later, he moved to Schenectady, New York, to work at General Motors, and soon returned to Stanford University to complete his Master of Science degree in electrical engineering. In 1938, Dave Packard and Lucile Salter were married. The couple had four children out of their union, David, Nancy, Susan and Julie.

The newlyweds moved into the home that would be associated with the "HP Garage". The home was owned by Dr. Spencer, Palo Alto's first mayor, and his wife. After Dr. Spencer passed away, Mrs. Spencer retreated to the second story apartment, while the couple shared the three-room, first story apartment and Bill Hewlett often slept in the shed or what is now known as the "HP Garage".

HP Company
The HP Garage is considered the "birthplace of Silicon Valley". The Palo Alto home was the center of business for Dave Packard and William Redington Hewlett, where they spent long hours brainstorming and building innovative tools. The HP Garage is preserved in its exact location in its original format to this day and was, in 1987, designated as a California State historical landmark.

Originally the company sold a range of products including voltmeters, thermometers, audio processors, oscilloscopes, signal generators, frequency meters, time standards and wave analyzers among others. They also created electronic instruments for agricultural use, athletic game equipment and more.

The first product that was a true sales success was the HP

200A Precision Model Audio Oscillator. They sold 8 copies of its improved model, the 200B, to Walt Disney to test his Fanta sound Surround Sound. Hewlett and Packard creatively designed a model that was able to stabilize the amplitude of the sounds using a small light bulb.

The pair were mentored by their professor and one of "the Fathers of Silicon Valley", Fred Terman. Fred Terman had a passion for radio engineering and was well acquainted with many of the radio companies and major pioneers of the industry.

Terman introduced Hewlett and Packard to many of his connections and encouraged them to go into business together. They used their connections to build better products, working with inventors, like Charlie Litton, often using his engraving equipment to brand their creations. The relationship amongst competitors at that time was often friendly and non-competitive, setting the foundation for some of the key players of the technology industries to follow.

As the company grew in profits, Hewlett and Packard made the decision to expand out of the garage. The company had reached a stage where they required more employees. In addition, Hewlett would be married to Flora Lamson and desired a more comfortable quarters to bring his bride home.

Shortly thereafter, Bill Hewlett was called to serve in World War II. With the outbreak of war, and like many other US based companies, sales soared for the Hewlett-Packard Company.

The HP Company expanded into Stanford Research Park which had been established by their mentor, Fred Terman, to encourage a technological presence near the university. Hewlett and Packard encouraged a positive work environment that employees could enjoy and would also foster creativity and innovation. They were keen to interact with all of their employees and were often seen as the grill masters for company barbecues. They also encouraged employees by the payment of regular bonuses. Hewlett and Packard held an excellent reputation within their company and their positive employee friendly style of management became known as "The HP Way". Bill Hewlett defined the HP Way as being "a core ideology ... which includes a deep respect for the individual, a dedication to affordable quality and reliability, a commitment to community responsibility, and a view that the company exists to make technical contributions for the advancement and welfare of humanity."

Dave Packard and Bill Hewlett had a great working relationship, often shifting the responsibility from one partner to the other. For example, when Bill Hewlett was enrolled in the Army, Dave Packard quickly took the lead, even limiting his salary to match Hewlett's military pay.

Dave Packard went on to serve the United States Government, appointed by Richard Nixon to be the Deputy Secretary of Defense in 1969.

In 1966 HP entered the computer market with the HP 2100A. This proved to be a key move on HP's part, as HP was credited, by *Wired* magazine, with creating the first device to be designated as a "personal computer". The HP company is renowned for its quality electronic products and innovation, also inventing the first scientific electronic calculator and the first handheld programmable in 1974.

In later years the company continued to grow, focusing not only on a wide range of IT products from printers, to computers, to servers and networking hardware but also becoming one of the leading global supplier of IT services.

Dave Packard with his wife Lucile, founded the David and Lucile Packard Foundation in 1964. Its stated goals on its website are to "improve the lives of children, enable creative pursuit of science, advance reproductive health, and conserve and restore earth's natural systems". As of 2004 an audit by Deloitte & Touche reported that the foundation had total assets of $5.4 billion.

Bill Hewlett, with his wife Flora also established a charitable foundation two years later in 1966 that supports educational and cultural institutions and also looks to advance specific social and environmental issues[193]. As of 2011 the foundation had assets of over $7 billion and awarded a total of $202 million grants and £353 million in grant and gift payments in that same year.

Bill Hewlett and Dave Packard died in 2001 and 1996 respectively. They leave behind not only one of the world's leading IT companies but also a significant charitable legacy.

5. Steve Jobs, co-founder of Apple

Overview
Steve Jobs was an entrepreneur, innovator and the co-founder of Apple, the world's most iconic information technology company. Steve Jobs is credited for his groundbreaking success with the creation of the Mac, iPhone, iPod, iTunes store and the iPad. His innovation continually astounded the computer technology industry, setting high standards of beauty, simplicity, creativity and function that competitors could only aspire to.

Early Years
Steve Jobs came into the world on February the 24th 1955 but wasn't born under traditional circumstances. His mother, Joanne Carloe Schieble, was a Swiss-American

Catholic student and his father, Abdulfattah "John" Jandali, was a young Syrian political science professor who met at the University of Wisconsin. After Steve was born they decided not to keep Steve, primarily because Joanne's family disapproved of the relationship.

Steve Jobs was adopted by Paul and Clara Jobs, a middle-income family in San Francisco, California. The family moved to Mountain View, California. Steve Jobs' adoptive father, who he firmly referred to as his "father", worked as a carpenter and a mechanic, fostering Jobs' interest in electronics. They often worked together in Jobs' garage, deconstructing and rebuilding radios and other electronics.

Clara Jobs worked as an accountant for one of the first high tech firms in Silicon Valley, Varian Enterprises. Steve Jobs grew up in Silicon Valley at a time when technology and the electronics industry was booming.

Despite his intelligence, throughout his school years, Steve Jobs habitually put more effort into playing pranks than studying. He was often in the center of trouble and had to be bribed to study for his tests. Despite this he managed to excel academically and, based on his test scores, his school offered to skip him two grades, but his parents declined. As a compromise they let him skip ahead one grade.

During one summer, Steve Jobs and his soon to be Apple co-founder Steve Wozniack, worked at Hewlett Packard. Upon high school graduation, Steve Jobs' parents made every effort to keep their promise to Steve Jobs' biological parents to send him to college. In spite of their limited income, Paul and Clara Jobs sent Steve to Reed College, a liberal arts college in eastern Oregon.

After only one semester, Steve Jobs quit school. He continued sitting in on various classes like auditing and calligraphy. In those days, he would often sleep on the dorm room floors of his friends. He earned money by trading in Coke bottles and ate free meals at the Hare Krishna temple.

After an excursion to India, Steve Jobs returned to Silicon Valley to work for Atari as a video game designer and technician. It was there that he reconnected with his friend, Steve Wozniak, and began attending "Homebrew Computer Club" meetings. In these meetings, fellow technicians and computer hobbyists gathered to share their latest discoveries, computer parts they had built and codes they had written. Steve Wozniak, known as "Woz", displayed his keen understanding of and love for computer technology and electronics though this club.

Jobs and "Woz" found a new way to make money by selling little "blue boxes", after learning about the technology in a magazine. The "blue boxes" would emulate telephone network sounds, allowing users to make free long distance calls. This endeavor proved to be eye-opening for Steve Jobs. Once he discovered that he could make something that could compete and even usurp large established industries, he began to look at the world differently.

The Birth of Apple
In 1976, the Apple I was born. Steve Wozniak created this innovation single-handedly for use as a personal computer. After Woz shared this technology with his friend, Jobs encouraged his partner, Woz, to sell these devices.

Steve Jobs and Steve Wozniak created the Apple Company together in Job's family's house garage for the purpose of selling the Apple 1 computer. Jobs named the computer and the company "Apple" after the time he had spent in a hippie community picking apples. They received funding from an Intel product marketing manager and engineer, Mike Markkula. As the company started to grow Jobs recruited top entrepreneurs in the industry including John Sculley of Pepsi-Cola and Mike Scott of National Semiconductor.

When Steve Jobs saw the then new graphical user interface that Xerox had developed he took the idea, had the design elaborated, and then released the Apple Lisa computer that made use of it. Lisa was also the name of his first daughter, born in 1978, whom he had with his on-and-off girlfriend Chrisann Brennan. For the first two years of her life, Steve Jobs denied paternity claiming he was sterile, forcing the mother and daughter to live on welfare. After this time he admitted to being her father. His public persona as a creative genius often contrasted with his personal reputation which was significantly less flattering.

With a number of successful products Steve Jobs and his partner, Steve Wozniak quickly grew Apple into a multimillion dollar company. The Apple computers continually improved from the initial Apple I to the Lisa to the Macintosh. In all of his brilliance, Steve Jobs was notorious for his erratic behavior. After a shipping company failed to deliver some Apple computers in the specified space of time, Jobs instructed Apple to break the contract with the shipping company, in spite of a potential lawsuit. This kind of autocratic behavior upset board members, leading to Jobs' removal from his managerial duties. Jobs resigned from Apple a few months later.

In 1986, Steve Jobs bought The Graphics Group Company, later renamed Pixar for $10 million dollars. In partnership with Disney, Pixar produced hugely successful animated films such as *Toy Story, The Incredibles, A Bug's Life, Ratatouille, Finding Nemo* and others, winning multiple Academy Awards for Best Animated Feature. In 2006 Disney did an all stock purchase of Pixar, valuing the company at $7.4 billion. This left Steve Jobs as the single largest shareholder in the Disney Company at 7%, far exceeding the stock of Ron Disney.

During his time away from Apple, Steve Jobs founded NeXT Inc. in 1985 and in 1990 released the NeXT computer. The NeXT computer had extremely innovative capabilities and new technology such as a built-in Ethernet port, the digital signal processor chip and the Mach Kernel. This computer had the capability to share voice, image and text via the NeXT Mail multimedia email system.

However the NeXT computer was costly to produce and was too expensive to achieve the volume of sales required to make the business profitable. A number of units were sold and Sir Tim Berners-Lee invented the World Wide Web using a NeXT computer at the CERN institute in Europe. The true value of the NeXT Inc. Company lay in its innovative software. After several failed attempts to create a cost-effective product for the appropriate market, Jobs received an offer from Apple to buy the company and thus all its technologies and software for $427 million. This brought Jobs back into the company, officially in the capacity of an adviser.

After many transitional changes in leadership and a significant decline in the company's fortunes, Steve Jobs regained the position of CEO of Apple in 1997.

Under Steve Jobs' leadership, Apple entered the music industry, dominating digital downloads with the iPod. The iPod was the innovative digital music player that led to the demise of CD players and Walkmans. The iPod worked in partnership with Apple's flagship virtual store and content library system called iTunes. Controlling both the platform and the content delivery allowed Apple to make record profits and to make it into one of the most influential players in the music industry.

In June 2007, Apple entered the mobile phone market with the launch of the iPhone, revolutionizing the mobile phone market with its ergonomic design and application based operating system. The true appeal of the iPhone lay in its ability to run applications, or apps as they have become known, from both Apple and third parties. This has allowed the iPhone to become a versatile device used by people to do everything from check their emails, plan a journey, update their social media status, make banking transactions, take pictures and even text and ring people. Having a so called smart phone has become an essential tool in the developed world.

In 2010 Apple launched the iPad, another disruptive and innovative product that transformed the tablet market, creating another significant and highly profitable revenue stream for Apple.

The unprecedented success of the iPod, the iPhone, the iPad and other Apple products and services led to Apple becoming, by market capitalization, the biggest company in the world and also one of the most profitable.

On October the 5th 2011, Steve Jobs died of pancreatic cancer, only a few months after resigning his duties at Apple.

Apple has become synonymous with creativity, innovation, design and quality. Apple led the personal computer and device revolution but it remains to be seen if it can continue to deliver the same innovations and success now that the Steve Jobs era is over.

6. Alan Turing

A plaque beneath a statue in Sackville Park in Manchester, England states:

Alan Mathison Turing
1912-1954
Father of Computer Science
Mathematician, Logician
Wartime Codebreaker
Victim of Prejudice

The statue shows Turing, who worked in Manchester near the end of his life, eating an apple, often a symbol of forbidden knowledge. The apple also represents the method of poisoning Turing used to take his own life. It was a life filled with accomplishments and disgrace and one that gave the world many of the foundations of computer science.

When it included Turing on its list of the 100 Most Important People of the 20th century, Time magazine stated: "The fact remains that everyone who taps at a keyboard, opening a spreadsheet or a word-processing program, is working on an incarnation of a Turing machine."

Turing also created a test, commonly called the Turing Test, which is used to determine artificial intelligence. In the Turing Test, a person asks questions of both a computer and a human participant -- both unseen -- to try to determine which one is the computer and which one is the human. If the computer can fool the person, it is deemed intelligent.

In addition to his scientific achievements, Turing played a key role breaking the Enigma code used by Nazi Germany in World War II. Having access to secret German dispatches saved many allied lives and contributed to a number of German defeats during the war.

So how did someone so brilliant who contributed so much to society come to commit suicide at the age of 41? During

Turing's lifetime, homosexuality was considered a crime in England. He was convicted of "gross indecency" and, as an alternative to a lengthy prison term, he was sentenced to chemical castration by a series of hormone injections. The criminal conviction cost him his career and his reputation.

Turing was born in London in 1912 to Julius and Ethel Turing while his father was on an extended leave from his job with the Indian Civil Service. Since their parents wanted their children to be brought up in England, Turing and his older brother, John, were left in the care of a retired Army couple when they returned to serve in India.

As a child, Turing displayed a natural talent for learning and for mathematics and science in particular. When his first day at the Sherborne School coincided with the 1926 General Strike in Britain, the 13-year-old was so determined to attend school that he cycled over 60 miles on his bicycle to ensure he could attend class.

At Sherborne, Turing was able to grasp and solve advanced problems without having studied elementary calculus. At a school devoted to the classics, his scientific brain was not always appreciated. A letter from his headmaster to his parents stated: "If he is to stay at public school, he must aim at becoming educated. If he is to be solely a Scientific Specialist, he is wasting his time at a public school."

Turing went on to study mathematics at Cambridge University and upon graduation taught there in the new and growing field of quantum mechanics. It was at Cambridge that he developed the concept, which later became referred to as the Turing machine, which is now thought of as the basis of modern computing.

The Turing machine manipulates symbols on a strip of tape

as per a table of rules and can be adapted to simulate the logic of any computer algorithm. Turing called it an "a-machine" (automatic machine). It is useful in helping computer scientists understand the limits of mechanical computation.

In 1938, Turing began to work in secret on a part-time basis for England's Government Code and Cypher School, and, when the Second World War commenced, he worked full-time work at the school's headquarters in Bletchley Park.

There he led the team responsible for deciphering the messages encrypted by the German Enigma machine. The team designed an electromechanical machine known as a "bombe" that successfully decoded German messages; this work was critical in the war effort for the Allies. The bombe was used to discover some of the daily settings of the German Enigma machines, including the set of rotors in use and their positions in the machine and the rotor core start positions for the coded messages.

After the war, Turing's work at Bletchley Park motivated him to develop a machine that would logically process information. At the National Physical Laboratory (NPL), however, his plans, which if completed upon his specifications could have become the first complete electronic stored-program digital computer, were dismissed by his colleagues as being too difficult to even attempt. Had Turing's computer been built as planned, it would have had run faster and had more memory than any of the other early computers.

Discouraged by the delays at NPL, Turing began work as director of the computing laboratory at Manchester University. He designed the programming system of the Ferranti Mark I, the world's first commercially available electronic digital computer. Also at Manchester, Turing began his work on artificial intelligence, and he put forth the theory that the human brain is essentially a digital computing machine.

In 1952, after Turing reported a home burglary to police, he was forced to reveal that he was involved in a homosexual relationship. He was then arrested and tried for what was considered a criminal offence in England at the time. To avoid a prison sentence, Turing accepted injections of estrogen for the period of a year.

Since the English government considered homosexuals to be susceptible to blackmail and therefore a security risk, Turing's security clearance was revoked, meaning he could no longer do his work. On June 8, 1954, Turing's housecleaner found him dead. A post-mortem examination established cyanide poisoning as the cause of death. A half-eaten apple lay beside Turing's bed when he was found, and although the apple was never tested, it was believed to have been tainted with the poison.

Turing's life has been the subject of the 1986 play by Hugh Whitemore, "Breaking the Code," as well as several biographies. His biographers Andrew Hodges and David Leavitt suggest that Turing re-enacted a scene from Walt Disney's 1937 animated film *Snow White* in eating a poisonous apple. Turing's friend, Alan Garner, supported this theory in an article published in The Guardian in 2011.

This was a tragic end to a life cut short of a great man who contributed much to the allied cause in the Second World War and also to the worlds of science and computing. In 2009 Alan Turing received an official public apology on behalf of the British government for "the appalling way he was treated." In 2013 Alan Turing also received a posthumous pardon under the royal prerogative of mercy[194] from the British government.

7. William (Bill) Henry Gates III

"Success is a lousy teacher. It seduces smart people into thinking they can't lose." – Bill Gates

Bill Gates should know about success. Along with the late Steve Jobs, his is one of the most recognizable names in the business world. As the co-founder of Microsoft, Gates built the world's largest software company and made himself one of the richest men in the world.

Although he transitioned out of his hands-on role in the daily operation of Microsoft in 2008 in order to devote more time to his charitable work, Gates continues to serve as Microsoft's chairman.

Born in 1955 in Seattle, Washington, Gates and his two sisters are the children of William Gates, a lawyer, and Mary Gates, a teacher. Although his parents had a career in law in mind for him, from age 13 Gates showed an interest in computer programming when he was a student at the Lakeside School, an exclusive Seattle preparatory school. He took a keen interest in programming the school's new GE system in BASIC computer, to such an extent that he even found a way to be excused from math classes to spend more time on the system.

Gates used this school computer to write his first computer program, a tic-tac-toe game. Following this he and a few other students – one of whom was Paul Allen – began to look for ways to spend more time on other computers, including a PDP-10 belonging to Computer Center Corporation (CCC). CCC ending up banning the students for the summer after it caught them manipulating the operating system in order to obtain free computer time.

After school administrators learned of Gates's programming abilities, they asked him to write the computer program for their students' class schedules. Gates later recalled he changed the code to ensure he shared classes with "a disproportionate number of interesting girls."

At the age of 15, Gates and his friend, Paul Allen, created Traf-O-Data, a computer program company that counted traffic and was based on the Intel 8008 processor. While the company eventually flopped, Gates and Allen have both said they used much of the trial and error knowledge they learned from Traf-o-Data later when they created Microsoft several years later.

Gates enrolled at Harvard University in 1973, but he tended to spend more time in the computer room than in class. He remained in contact with Allen, and the two young men both worked at Honeywell the following summer. After the software that they wrote and designed for an MITS Altair computer was a success, Gates decided to leave Harvard and join Allen in forming their own business. In 1975, they created Micro-Soft (later dropping the hyphen).

At this time, computer hobbyists were openly copying and sharing software. Gates said in a later interview that he found that only about 10 percent of the people using Microsoft's BASIC in the Altair computer had actually bought it. In 1976, he wrote an open letter to consumers stating that the stealing of software would result in less innovation in the long run.

After Microsoft's relationship with MITS ended on an unfriendly note, Gates and Allen moved their company operations to Bellevue, Washington, just east of Seattle. By the end of 1978, with 23-year-old Gates at the helm, Microsoft had 25 employees and a gross of $2.5 million.

When IBM wanted to create a new personal computer that

was affordable for home and small business use, the company looked to Microsoft. Although IBM wanted to buy the source code in its entirety, Gates instead suggested IBM pay a licensing fee for each copy of the software that came installed or bundled with their computers. Microsoft, therefore, was able to license its MS-DOS software to any other PC manufacturer. This proved to be a key business decision when other computer companies began to copy the IBM PC.

In 1981 Gates and Allen incorporated Microsoft. Gates became president and chairman of the board, and Allen became vice-president. By 1983, Microsoft grew, with staff numbers rising to 128, and revenues quadrupled from $4 million to $16 million. The company also went international with offices in Japan and the United Kingdom.

The same year also saw Allen's diagnosis with Hodgkin's disease. Although he went into remission after extensive treatment, Allen resigned from Microsoft.

By this time, competition in the computer business was fierce, with Microsoft and Apple going head to head for customers. In November 1985, Microsoft launched Windows, a system that was very similar to the Apple Macintosh system that had been released nearly two years earlier. Although Apple sued Microsoft for copyright infringement, the court ruled in favour of Microsoft, stating that while there were indeed similarities in the way the two software systems operated, each individual function was different.

Gates took Microsoft public in 1986 with an initial public offering of $21 per share. He held 45 percent of the 24.7 million shares and became a millionaire at the age of 31. In 1987, he became a billionaire when the stock reached $90.75 a share. Since achieving billionaire status Gates has been identified either as one of the and, more often than not, the wealthiest American by Forbes magazine's annual list of the top 400 wealthiest people in America.

Gates co-wrote the book *The Road Ahead* in 1995, which stayed at the top of the New York Times bestseller list for seven weeks. His 1999 book, *Business @ the Speed of Thought*, which details his thoughts on how technology can solve business problems, was translated into 25 languages and also made it to the top of the *Times* bestseller list.

As Gates's wealth increased so did his interest in philanthropy. He donated the proceeds of both of these books to non-profit organizations that promote the use of technology in the field of education. He and his wife, Melinda, started the William H. Gates Foundation soon after their marriage in 1994. In 2000, they combined several charitable projects into one by forming the Bill and Melinda Gates Foundation, starting it off with a $28 billion personal contribution.

In addition to his own charitable giving he has been successful in encouraging other rich people to give away large parts of their fortunes to progressive charitable causes and his own foundation.

As of 2014 Gates, whose net worth is estimated by *Forbes* as $72 billion, works full time for the foundation, which focuses on extreme poverty and poor health conditions in developing countries. He writes regularly about foundation projects on Gates Notes, a website he launched in early 2010.

Gates and his wife have three children. He enjoys reading, playing golf, tennis and bridge. The family lives in a 55,000 square foot house on the shore of Lake Washington.

Although he dropped out of Harvard, Gates holds honorary doctorates from several universities and an honorary

Knight Commander of the Order of the British Empire from Queen Elizabeth II. For their philanthropic work the Mexican government awarded Bill and Melinda Gates the Order of the Aztec Eagle.

8. Don Estridge: The Father of the IBM PC

True to his training as an engineer, the first thing Phillip Donald (Don) Estridge did when he was assigned the task of developing a low-cost personal computer for IBM in 1980, was to buy the current offerings on the market – those from Apple, Commodore and Radio Shack – and take them apart in his office. He then challenged himself and his team members to do better.

With the code-name Acorn, a relatively small budget and a dozen or so engineers, Estridge was in charge of a small "skunk-works" called Entry Level Systems based in then sleepy Boca Raton, Florida. By breaking or at least bending some rules, including going to outside vendors for hardware and software, Estridge led his team in developing the original IBM Personal Computer. The IBM PC set a new standard against which the entire computer industry had to compete, and Estridge justly earned the title of "The Father of the IBM PC."

Since IBM had traditionally done all its own technology development and had used all its own parts, Estridge's unabashed way of looking at the competition was definitely unexplored territory for the company. His unorthodox way of doing things resulted, however, in his team developing and rolling out the IBM PC in a year's time – which at the time was faster than any other product launch in IBM's history.

Before the PC, the best-selling IBM computer had sold 25,000 units. Estridge set an ambitious goal of 250,000 units. By 1985, a million units had sold, and the Entry Level System Division had 10,000 employees and a turnover of $4.5 billion.

"We didn't look closely at any single product," Estridge said in a 1982 interview with PC Magazine. "Instead, we looked closely at what purchasers were doing. We asked these kinds of questions: Why did the customers buy? What machine capabilities were the customers using? Why would people want to buy a personal computer in the future? If you hadn't purchased one yet, what was it you were waiting for?"

Don Estridge was born in 1937 in Jacksonville, Florida. After obtaining his BS in electrical engineering from the University of Florida in 1959, he joined IBM as a junior engineer. Early in his career he worked for the company's Federal Services Division, including programming support for NASA at the Goddard Space Flight Center near Washington, D.C. He and his family -- which by then included his wife, Mary Ann and their three daughters -- later moved to Boca Raton, where he joined IBM's General Systems Division and served as a programming manager for the IBM Series 1 mini-computer.

By 1980, IBM got serious about competing in the new and rapidly growing personal computer market and established what it called Entry Level Systems to research and develop an affordable computer for small business and personal use.

"There were a lot of people at IBM—not just in the technical areas, but throughout the company—who wanted IBM to build a personal computer," Estridge said in the PC Magazine interview. "There was a high level of enthusiasm; if you became a member of the project that enthusiasm carried over into the project.

"From the beginning, we knew that we wanted to build so we didn't spin our wheels asking, 'Is this the thing we really wanted to do?' I think it has already been shown that we were more on the track than off it. Then we just went to work—and didn't eat or sleep for a year."

By choosing other companies' parts "off the shelf" and opting for third party software, Estridge did something revolutionary in the computer world at the time. He made the IBM PC "open," enabling other manufacturers to build on what he and his team created by making the design specifications public knowledge.

According to an August 1981 IBM press release introducing its new PC: "Designed for business, school and home, the easy-to-use system sells for as little as $1,565... IBM has designed its Personal Computer for the first-time or advanced user, whether a businessperson in need of accounting help or a student preparing a term paper."

The first IBM PC was sold at Computer Land stores, at Sears, Roebuck and Co., through IBM Product Centers and through a special sales unit in the company's data processing division.

"We didn't think we could introduce a product that could out-BASIC Microsoft's BASIC," he said in the PC interview. "We would have to out-BASIC Microsoft and out-VisiCalc VisiCorp and out-Peachtree Peachtree - and you just can't do that."

According to several biographies, Estridge turned down a multi-million dollar offer in 1983 from Steve Jobs to become the president of Apple Computer. Fiercely loyal to IBM, Estridge may have been given a similar offer from Bill Gates of Microsoft, with whom he had a good business relationship, according to the same sources.

Estridge's long-time friend and colleague Jan Winston told The History of the Computing Project (www.thocp.net) that Estridgo was a humble man with a good sense of humor.

"He combined a manic drive with tremendous respect for his people, recognizing all that they were sacrificing during the PC project," Winston recalled. "When the PC took off, it was like a rocket ride, and he did a wonderful job of exerting executive leadership. And he was a technically competent visionary. Don had a very broad view of where computer business was going technically as well as the importance of computers to the economy and to society as a whole."

Estridge was appointed president of the by-then booming Entry Systems Division in 1983 and was made a vice president of IBM in January 1984. He had responsibility for world-wide development and product management and for U.S. manufacturing.

Estridge, 48, and his wife were killed on Aug. 2, 1985 in plane crash near Dallas, Texas. According to official reports, the Delta flight was the victim of "wind shear," but some reports attribute the crash ironically to a failed computer system at flight control.

At the time IBM President and CEO John F. Akers said, "Don Estridge was a man of vision whose skill and leadership helped guide IBM's personal computer business to success. He had a very bright future in our business. He and Mary Ann will be greatly missed by all their friends and colleagues."

Despite his visionary leadership, even Estridge could not foresee the vast technological changes that were ahead. At the West Coast Computer Faire in San Francisco in 1982, Estridge led a session for software designers and hardware vendors and said, "There's a question that keeps coming up like waves on the beach: 'What do I use one for?'"

His friend Winston put it this way: "We always said to ourselves that the technology would grow by leaps and bounds because of applications like VisiCalc. We knew there was going to be e-mail too.

"But the broad acceptance of the computer, the way it embedded itself in our everyday lives and the explosion of the Internet, is an order of magnitude beyond what we were thinking about in the early '80s."

In 1999, Estridge was called "one of the people who "invented the enterprise" by CIO Magazine. The former IBM Facility Building 051 in Boca Raton is now the Don Estridge High-Tech Middle School. At its dedication in 2005, Estridge's family donated his own personal IBM 5150 computer to the school.

9. H. Ross Perot

Although many people might recognize Ross Perot's name as a two-time third-party U.S. presidential candidate, politics is just one part of his long and colourful career.

Among other things, the feisty octogenarian built his own leading IT services company Electronic Data Systems (EDS), recruited and sponsored a mission to rescue two EDS employees from Iran, worked to find and free Vietnam POW/MIAs, and made a fortune selling EDS to General Motors, founding another company, Ross Systems, and selling it to Dell Inc. In addition, Perot, whose net worth is estimated to be $3.5 billion, founded the Perot Foundation, which has donated some $200 million to charity.

Perot was born in 1930 in Texarkana, Texas, to Gabriel

Ross Perot, who ran a cotton wholesaling company , and Lulu May (Ray) Perot who was a secretary. He officially changed his name from Henry Ray Perot to Henry Ross Perot when he was 12 so that he could be called Ross like his father. As a child, he often went along with his father to cattle auctions, and he later told biographer Ken Gross that it was during this period that he picked up many of his salesmanship skills.

Beginning at the age of seven, he took on all sorts of jobs, including selling magazine subscriptions, garden seeds and greetings cards door-to-door. As a teen, he bought and sold saddles and other animal equipment and sometimes the animals as well. "I was what they called a day trader," Perot once recalled in an interview. "You'd buy it in the morning and sell it in the afternoon and make a few dollars' profit if you were lucky."

Perot attended public school and Texarkana Junior College before entering the United States Naval Academy in 1949 and graduating in 1953. While at Annapolis, he served as class president in both his junior and senior year, chairman of the honour committee and battalion commander.

He met his future wife, Margot, while at the Naval Academy, and the two married in 1956. Deciding against a career in the military, Perot and his bride moved to Dallas after his discharge in 1957, and he got a job as a salesman for IBM's data processing division. The couple ended up having five children.

His skills as a salesman were put to good use, and Perot decided start his own company after a few years with IBM. With a $1,000 loan from his wife, who was working as a teacher at the time, Perot launched EDS in 1962. His pioneering IT company provided government and corporate businesses with data processing systems and services. Such was his belief and tenacity that it is said he received seventy seven no's for his fledgling company's services before he won his first contract.

Although it started out as a one-man operation, EDS grew to become a multi-billion dollar corporation with more than 70,000 employees. The creation of Medicare in 1965 allowed EDS to start bidding for new government contracts, and by 1968 Medicare and Medicaid contracts provided about one-fourth of all EDS revenues. Fortune magazine placed Perot on its cover in 1968 and called him the "fastest, richest Texan."

In the 1970s, Perot became interested in the issue of Vietnam War prisoners of war and missing in action soldiers and travelled to Vietnam on their behalf multiple times. In 1974, the Department of Defense awarded him the Medal for Distinguished Public Service for his efforts on behalf of POWs.

When two EDS employees were taken hostage in Iran in late 1978, Perot recruited, financed and sent a team of military veterans in a covert mission called Operation Hotfoot to rescue them. The mission would later be told in Ken Follett's book *On Wings of Eagles*. The dramatic story was made into a 1986 TV mini-series with actor Richard Crenna portraying Ross Perot.

Perot sold controlling interest in EDS to General Motors in 1984 for $2.5 billion and GM shares, making him GM's largest shareholder and a director of the company, while remaining CEO of EDS. Two years later he sold his GM stock back to the company for nearly $750 million and resigned from the GM board.

He soon invested his profits in a new computer services business, Perot Systems. Perot turned the day-to-day operations of Perot Systems over to his son, Ross, Jr., in 2000. In 2009 Perot sold the business to Dell Inc. for $3.9

billion.

Always outspoken in his political views, Perot decided to get more directly involved in politics in the presidential campaign of 1992. He discussed his ideas for rebuilding America in his book *United We Stand: How We Can Take Back Our Country* and used his wealth to purchase television commercials to promote himself and his ideas. His campaign gained momentum and at one stage he led in the polls. In July 1992, he dropped out of the race and later claimed this was because the George H.W. Bush campaign had threatened to run a smear campaign about his daughter's sexuality who was about to get married.

Despite the initial withdrawal, when he did an about turn and returned to the race in October of that same year, Perot went on to win around 19 percent of the popular vote, the first independent candidate since Teddy Roosevelt in 1912 to receive such a large share of the total number of votes cast. When Bill Clinton, who was a democrat, won the election, many Republicans blamed Perot for the loss. Perot launched another candidacy against Clinton four years later, but that campaign failed to capture widespread support.

Perot has written several books, including *Ross Perot: My Life & the Principles for Success*; *Not for Sale at Any Price*; *Save Your Job, Save Our Country*; *Preparing Our Country for the 21st Century*; and *Ross Perot: My Life.*

He and his family are active philanthropists, having donated more $100 million to civil, social and charitable causes. In 2008, the five Perot children gave, in honour of their parents, a $50 million gift to the Museum of Nature & Science in Dallas. The museum named a new dinosaur species after the Perot family; it is Pachyrhinosaurus perotorum. The Perot Museum of Nature & Science opened at Dallas' Victory Park location opened in 2012.

As of his eighty third birthday, Perot continues to stay active and reportedly wears a suit and tie every day. "The world wants things done, not excuses," he told Forbes magazine in an interview. "One thing done well is worth a million good excuses."

10. Larry Page and Sergey Brin

- goo·gle transitive verb, often capitalized \'gü-gəl\
  goo·gled   goo·gling
  Definition: to use the Google search engine to obtain information about (as a person) on the World Wide Web.

You know you've created something pretty noteworthy when its name becomes a new word in the dictionary. The word "google" was added to the Merriam-Webster Collegiate Dictionary and to the Oxford Dictionary of English in 2006. Prior to that, the American Dialect Society chose it as the "most useful word" of 2002.

As anyone who uses the Internet knows, to "google" someone or something means to use the massive search engine of the same name. Founded in 1998 by Larry Page and Sergey Brin, Google's trademarked name is a creative spelling of the word "googol," which means a number equal to 10 to the 100th power or, colloquially, a big number.

Google co-founder Page may have been the first to use the name of his company as a verb when he wrote "Have fun and keep googling" on an early mailing list in 1998. Today Google is a multinational corporation offering Internet services including search, cloud computing, software and online advertising technologies based in Mountain View, California. Most of its income is derived from advertising.

Founded in September 1998 as a privately-held company, Page and Brin made an initial public offering of Google in August 2004. Together the two men retain ownership of about 16 percent of its shares.

Google's mission statement is to "organize the world's information and make it universally accessible and useful," but it started out as a research project Page and Brin were working on as Ph.D. students at Stanford University in 1996.

Convention for search engines at this time was for them to rank results based on how many times the terms that were being searched for appeared on each page. The two students began to theorize about a system that would instead analyze the relationships between websites. They named this new approach "PageRank," seeing as it determined the relevance of a website by a combination of the number of pages and also the relative importance of the pages that were linked to it.

They first called their new search engine "Backrub" because it used backlinks to evaluate the importance of a website. The name "Google" better signified the large quantities of information the search engine could analyse, and Google first ran under the Stanford website, with the domain name google.stanford.edu.

Brin and Page met in March 1995 when Brin, who had been in the Stanford Ph.D. program for two years, was detailed to escort some new candidates, including Page, around the campus.

Later Brin, who had not settled on a research project yet, was intrigued by Page's BackRub premise. "I talked to lots of research groups," he recalled later in an interview, "and this was the most exciting project, both because it tackled the Web, which represents human knowledge, and because I liked Larry."

In an interview with *The Economist* magazine, Brin said, "We're both kind of obnoxious." He also said the two men disagreed on most subjects but still "became intellectual soul-mates and close friends."

Combining their talents, Page and Brin began filling their dormitory room with inexpensive computers and testing their new search engine design. Their project, which resulted in the paper titled "The Anatomy of a Large-Scale Hypertextual Web Search Engine," soon grew large enough to tax the Stanford computer infrastructure. The young men realized they were onto something big and began to solicit funds from faculty members, family and friends to expand their research in a rented garage. In fact, when Andy Bechtolsheim, co-founder of Sun Microsystems, wrote a cheque for $100,000 to "Google, Inc.", Google hadn't even been incorporated yet.

Sergey Mikhaylovich Brin, whose personal wealth today is estimated at more than $24 billion, was born in Moscow in 1973 to Russian Jewish parents, Michael Brin and Eugenia Brin, who were both graduates of Moscow State University. When Brin was small, he lived in a three-room apartment with his parents and his grandmother.

The Brin family immigrated to the United States to escape Jewish persecution when Brin was six. In an interview in 2000, Brin said, "I know the hard times that my parents went through there (the Soviet Union) and I am very thankful that I was brought to the States." His father became a professor of mathematics at the University of Maryland, and his mother a researcher at NASA's Goddard Space Flight Center near Washington, D.C.

Brin attended a Maryland Montessori school for his

elementary education and graduated from Eleanor Roosevelt High School in Greenbelt, Maryland.Brin followed in the footsteps of both his father and his grandfather by studying mathematics, and he earned his undergraduate degree from the University of Maryland. After graduation, Brin enrolled at Stanford to begin his graduate studies in computer science on a graduate fellowship from the National Science Foundation.

Brin and his wife, Anne Wojcicki, who is co-founder and CEO of 23andMe, which provides ancestry-related genetic reports and raw genetic data, were married in 2007. Brin and Wojcicki are the parents of two children.

Brin currently serves as director of special projects for Google, and continues to share decision making for the company with Page, Google's CEO, and with Eric Schmidt, who is executive chairman.

Lawrence "Larry" Page was born in 1973 in East Lansing, Michigan and is the son of Carl and Gloria Page, two early computer scientists. His father is recognized as being a pioneer in artificial intelligence and computer science and both his parents were computer science professors at Michigan State University.

Like Brin, Page also attended a Montessori school for grade school, and he graduated in 1991 from East Lansing High School. He earned a B.S. in computer engineering from the University of Michigan with honours and his Master's in computer science from Stanford University.

Recalling his childhood, Page said in an interview that his house "was usually a mess, with computers and *Popular Science* magazines all over the place." He noted that he was first kid in his elementary school to turn in an assignment printed from a word processor.

He and his older brother enjoyed taking things apart, and he said that he knew by the age of 12 that he wanted to "invent things" and have his own company. For the computer science Ph.D. program at Stanford, Page considered exploring the World Wide Web's mathematical properties. Page focused on the problem of finding out which web pages link to a given page, reasoning that if he could create a method to count and qualify each backlink, the Web would become more useful and valuable. At the time Page started the project, the Web consisted of an estimated 10 million documents, with an unknown number of links between them. He created PageRank, which became the foundation of the search engine he devised with Brin.

Page, who Forbes estimates to be worth $24.9 billion, married research scientist Lucinda Southworth in 2007, and they are the parents of two children.

Both Brin and Page have used their wealth – both individually and collectively -- for philanthropic purposes. With a starting fund of $1 billion, they formed a non-profit charitable wing of Google called Google.org in 2004. The organization focuses on issues such as climate change, global public health, global poverty and renewable energy. For example, Page and Brin are investors in Tesla Motors, and they promote the adoption of hybrid electric cars. They also have invested in offshore wind power development. Other investment areas the Google founders share include: Space Adventures, the Virginia-based space tourism company; the Project Glass program, which is developing reality head-mounted displays; and a driverless car project.

Google is part of the Alliance for Affordable Internet (A4AI), a coalition of public and private organizations that are working to make the Internet access more affordable and accessible in developing countries.

With its ongoing corporate philosophies that include phrases such as "you can make money without doing evil," "you can be serious without a suit," and "work should be challenging and the challenge should be fun," Google consistently ranks as one of the top employers.

Google engineers are encouraged to use "Innovation Time Off," by spending 20 percent of their work time on projects that particularly interest them. This is not a totally altruistic approach by the company as these projects are all the intellectual property of the company and not the individual.Google claims that successful products such as Gmail, Google News, Orkut and AdSense originated from these independent projects.

Google's Mountain View, California headquarters, called "the Googleplex," offers sports and recreational amenities such as a track, workout rooms, rowing machines, a massage room, table football, billiard tables and ping pong, free to all employees.

According to the company website, Google has offices in more than 60 countries, maintains more than 180 Internet domains, and serves more than half of its results to people living outside the United States. It offers search interfaces in more than 130 languages, giving users the ability to restrict results to content written in their own language.

Larry Page once defined the perfect search engine as one that "understands exactly what you mean and gives you back exactly what you want." Since then Google has grown to offer numerous products beyond being just a search engine, from the Google Chrome browser to Gmail to hardware such as a mobile phone and a computer, but the search for information remains at the heart of the company. "Our goal is to make it as easy as possible for you to find the information you need and get the things you need to do done," pledges the company website.

In announcing Page and Brin as winners of Columbia University's Marconi Foundation Prize in 2004, John Jay Iselin congratulated them for an invention that has "fundamentally changed the way information is retrieved today." And if you don't believe me, you can google it.

11. The Father of the Computer: Charles Babbage

If you ask most people who invented the computer, you will get anything from a blank stare to the names of Alan Turing or Steve Jobs. Some particularly astute respondents may even mention William Oughtred who invented the slide rule way back in the early 17th century. However, most historians give the title "Father of the Computer" to British mathematician and inventor Charles Babbage.

In the years between 1833 and 1871, Babbage conceived and designed the Analytical Engine, a huge machine that used punched cards to perform calculations. The machine's two-part engine comprised what were referred to as the mill and the store. The mill, which can be considered the equivalent of a contemporary processor, operated on values retrieved from the store, which today we would call its memory. This invention was the world's first general-purpose computer.

Although Babbage was never able to complete the actual building of his Engine (because of its cost and political disagreements), his detailed plans enabled the Science Museum in London to build it more than a century later in 1991. Not surprisingly for those who had examined his work, the machine actually worked as he had predicted.

Born in London in 1791, Babbage was one of four children born to Benjamin Babbage, a banker, and Elizabeth Teape. He studied mathematics at Cambridge University and received an MA in 1817. Despite her family's objections, Babbage married Georgiana Whitmore in 1814, and the couple had eight children together

A natural mathematician, Babbage often found himself ahead of his teachers, and he co-founded the Analytical Society for reforming the mathematics of Newton taught at the time. As early as 1812, Babbage became pre-occupied with the idea of creating a machine to take the human error out of calculations.

Babbage presented a paper "Note on the application of machinery to the computation of astronomical and mathematical tables" that described a "difference engine" to the Royal Astronomical Society on June 14, 1822. In the paper he described the process of calculating polynomials by using a numerical method he called the differences method.

The Society approved the idea of his "difference engine," and in 1823 the government gave him a grant to aid in its construction of 1,500 English Pounds. To this end Babbage converted a room in his house into a workshop and, to help him construct the machine, hired Joseph Clement. The parts used in the construction were mostly custom parts that Babbage designed himself.

That year, Babbage published *On the Economy of Machinery and Manufacture,* the first publication on what today we call operations research.

Babbage's work was interrupted when during one tragic year – 1827 – he lost his wife, his father and two of his children. Already on the verge of a breakdown from overwork, Babbage took some friends' advice and took a trip through Europe to recuperate.

While Babbage was away from England, rumours spread that he was wasting the government's money and that even if he finished the machine that it had no real value. The Royal Society publicly defended the project and the government continued its financial support, but Babbage would continue to struggle with financial backing from that point on. He also began to have differences with Clement, who at one point refused to turn over the tools and drawings he was using to build the engine.

Babbage wrote in a letter in 1834, "The drawings and parts of the Engine are at length in a place of safety—I am almost worn out with disgust and annoyance at the whole affair." In 1842, the English government officially abandoned the project.

In the meantime, Babbage began to think about a different machine, an Analytical Engine, which could be programmed to perform any kind of mathematical calculation.

Although he devoted most of his time and much of the sizeable fortune he received from his father's estate towards the building of his Analytical Engine, Babbage never succeeded in completing any of his several designs for it. By all accounts, when he died at his home in London in 1871, he was a bitter and disappointed man.

His feelings are unfortunate since the man was undoubtedly a genius. In addition to his computer prototype designs, Babbage published six full-length works and nearly 90 papers and was a prolific inventor and visionary. Here are a few of his ideas and inventions:

- lighthouse signaling
- the ophthalmoscope

- the idea of black box recorders for railroads
- the use of tidal power
- a "cow-catcher" for the front of railway locomotives
- a tugboat for winching vessels upstream
- quick-release couplings for railway cars
- multi-colored theatre lighting
- an altimeter
- a seismic detector
- an arcade game version of tic-tac-toe
- a hydrofoil

Babbage also broke Vigenère's autokey cipher as well as a weaker cipher known as the Vigenère cipher, a discovery used by the English military in its foreign campaigns. Since it was not published for a few years, credit for this is often given to Friedrich Kasiski, but he broke the cipher several years after Babbage.

Although he was a sought-after party guest for his quick wit and story-telling ability, Babbage, who never re-married, had a temper and was regarded as somewhat eccentric in England. He was disappointed that while several European academies bestowed him with honours, the only honour his own country gave him during his lifetime was the Lucasian chair of mathematics at Cambridge.

The London Science Museum went on to build a second separate Difference Engine following Babbage's plans for the Difference Engine No 2. One is at the museum and the other, owned by the multi-millionaire Nathan Myhrvold, and is on exhibition in Mountain View, California at the Computer History Museum.

The London engine's first calculation returned results to 31 digits in 1991. In the year 2000 the printer Babbage had designed for the Difference Engine was also built the Science Museum.

In a letter he wrote late in his life, Babbage affirmed how he felt about his life's work: "If unwarned by my example, any man shall undertake and shall succeed in really constructing an engine ... upon different principles or by simpler mechanical means, I have no fear of leaving my reputation in his charge, for he alone will be fully able to appreciate the nature of my efforts and the value of their results."

12. Sir Tim Berners-Lee

He's been knighted by the queen.

He's been honoured at the opening ceremony of the Olympic Games.

He's been hailed by Time magazine as one of the 100 Greatest Minds of the 20th Century.

While people all over the world know the names of computer industry giants such as Bill Gates, Steve Jobs and Mark Zuckerberg, his is not a household name. Yet his invention literally changed the way we do everything from shopping, to working, to socializing and learning.

In 1989, Tim Berners-Lee used the Internet to create the World Wide Web. The Web, as it is known for short, has since become the most extensive communication system the world has ever known.

"I pieced it together as I pursued my regular work and personal life," Berners-Lee modestly explained in his 1999 book *Weaving the Web*. "But many other people, most of them unknown, contributed essential ingredients, in much the same almost random fashion. A group of individuals holding a common dream and working together at a distance brought about a great change."

Computers were part of Berners-Lee's life from the beginning. His parents, Conway Berners-Lee and Mary Lee Woods, worked on the Ferranti Mark 1, the first commercially-built computer. Born in London in 1955, Berners-Lee also learned about electronics from playing with a model railway as a boy. He went on to study physics at The Queen's College of the University of Oxford, and he earned a first-class degree in 1976.

While at Oxford, he assembled his first computer, using an M6800 processor, an old TV, a soldering iron and some TTL gates. According to at least one biographical source, Berners-Lee was, during his stay at Oxford, caught hacking and was denied access to the university's computer.

After graduation, Berners-Lee took his computer knowledge and his bent for tinkering with machines to Plessey Telecommunications, a UK Telecom equipment manufacturer, where he spent two years working on transaction systems, message relays and bar code technology. In 1978, he designed typesetting software for printers and worked on a multitasking operating system for D.G. Nash Ltd. For three years starting in 1981, he worked on technical design and communications software at John Poole's Image Computer Systems Ltd.

"He's a splendid and very intelligent man," noted former boss John Poole in an interview. "There are three parts to him: he is amenable and easy to talk to; he is very clever; and he is very dogged. Those things together are what have made him a success."

Berners-Lee began the development of what would become the World Wide Web while working as an independent consultant software engineer for CERN, an international scientific organization based in Geneva,

Switzerland.

Frustrated by the fact that every computer at CERN stored different information and each system required its own unique login-in to access the data, Berners-Lee worked to come up with a simpler means of managing and accessing the information. Although the program he devised, which he named "Enquire," was created for his own use and never published, it formed the framework for his later development of the World Wide Web.

Berners-Lee came up with the idea of sharing and organizing information that would be available from any system in any physical location by using a system of hyperlinks (virtual connections that "link" one piece of content to another) and Hypertext Transfer Protocol (HTTP), which acted as a way for systems to both receive and retrieve Web pages.

He also invented HTML (HyperText Markup Language), which is the standard programming language used by most web pages. In addition he invented the URL (Uniform Resource Locator) system that ensures that every Web page has a unique and non conflicting designation.

Berners-Lee said he chose the phrase "World Wide Web" for its alliteration and because the word "web" described his new system's decentralized global format.

"Creating the Web was really an act of desperation, because the situation without it was very difficult when I was working at CERN," Berners-Lee wrote. "Most of the technology involved in the Web, like the hypertext, like the Internet, multifont text objects, had all been designed already."

"I just had to put them together. It was a step of generalizing, going to a higher level of abstraction, thinking about all the documentation systems out there as being possibly part of a larger imaginary documentation system."

In December 1990 he made his "World Wide Web" program available throughout CERN, and released it on the wider Internet in mid-1991. Through 1991 and 1993, as the technologies and their use spread, Berners-Lee continued to work on the design of the Web, gaining and responding to feedback from users, and continually working to refine the specifications of URLs, HTTP and HTML.

In 1994, he founded the World Wide Web Consortium in an effort to develop technology and to enable the Web to reach its full potential. Today Berners-Lee serves as director of the Consortium, which has host sites located at a number of locations including the Massachusetts Institute of Technology (MIT) in the United States, the European Research Consortium for Informatics and Mathematics (ERCIM), and at Keio University in Japan.

He also is a director of the World Wide Web Foundation, which he started to help in the co-ordination and funding of efforts to further the Web to the greater benefit of humanity. Berners-Lee is committed to helping make sure the Web remains free and accessible so that people all over the globe can share knowledge and services in creative ways.

Berners-Lee has received world-wide recognition for his pioneering work. Most notably, in 2004, when he was knighted by Queen Elizabeth II. In addition, he was named a foreign associate of the United States National Academy of Sciences in 2009. He became the first holder of MIT's 3Com Founders Chair, is an Honorary Fellow of the Institute of Electrical and Electronics Engineers and is a Distinguished Fellow of the British Computer Society. In addition, he is both a member of the American Academy of Arts and Sciences and a Fellow of the British Royal

Society.

He appeared in person working with a now antiquated NeXT Computer (see the biographies of Steve Jobs and Ross Perot for more information on how the NeXT computer came about), the type of which he used when inventing the web, at the opening ceremony of the 2012 Summer Olympics at the London Olympic Stadium. Here he was hailed as the "Inventor of the World Wide Web." When he tweeted "This is for everyone," the words were instantly spelled out in LCD lights on chairs of the 80,000 people in attendance.

Berners-Lee advocates the use of the Internet as an advocate of freedom and is the president of the Open Data Institute. "Threats to the Internet, such as companies or governments that interfere with or snoop on Internet traffic, compromise basic human network rights," he said in a 2012 interview.

He helped to launch the Alliance for Affordable Internet (A4AI), a coalition of public and private organizations that includes Google, Facebook, Intel and Microsoft in 2013. The A4AI seeks to make the Internet more accessible and affordable in the developing world, where only one-third of people are online.

Berners-Lee appears to have kept some humor about his ground-breaking accomplishments. In a 2009 interview, he admitted that the pair of slashes ("//") he included in the design of web addresses were unnecessary. "There you go, it seemed like a good idea at the time," he said somewhat apologetically.

Probably the most impressive aspect of Berners-Lee's invention of the World Wide Web is that there are no patents on it, and he receives no royalties whatsoever from its use. "What impresses me was that he was not in it for the money," John Poole remarked. "That's his background: the academic side. His dream was a free interchange of Information, and he stood by his principles."

Berners-Lee, who is the father of two children, is protective of his and his family's privacy and turns down most interview requests.

"The Web is more a social creation than a technical one. I designed it for a social effect — to help people work together — and not as a technical toy," Berners-Lee wrote in Weaving the Web. "The ultimate goal of the Web is to support and improve our web like existence in the world. We clump into families, associations, and companies. We develop trust across the miles and distrust around the corner."

About the Author

Robin Fisher is recognised as one of the world's leading authorities on I.T. networking. He has more than 15 years of experience in internetworking and has provided IT services for several of the world's leading companies. He has numerous professional qualifications including the vendor agnostic CISSP, is a Microsoft Certified Systems Engineer and is also a Cisco Certified Security Professional and Internetworking Expert, registered No. 25298.

Robin can be reached at www.thebookonnetworks.com.

Resources

1 http://www.darpa.mil/About/History/History.aspx

2 https://history.state.gov/milestones/1953-1960/sputnik

3 http://www.internetsociety.org/internet/what-internet/history-internet/brief-history-internet

4 http://www.internetsociety.org/internet/what-internet/history-internet/brief-history-internet

5 http://www.cableorganizer.com/articles/fiber-optics-tutorial/history-production-fiber-optic.html

6 http://computer.howstuffworks.com/fiber-optic.htm

7 http://www.corp.att.com/history/milestone_1958.html

8 http://www.space.com/16549-telstar-satellite-first-tv-signal-anniversary.html

9 http://www.infoese.ca/History%20of%20Computing.html

10 http://www.britannica.com/EBchecked/topic/1461036/IBM-OS360

11 http://www.pcmag.com/encyclopedia/term/39698/circuit-switching

12 http://www.ll.mit.edu/about/History/60-innovations.pdf

13 http://computerguru.net/packetswitching

14 http://edition.cnn.com/TECH/computing/9907/06/1963.idg/

15 http://docs.lib.purdue.edu/cgi/viewcontent.cgi?

Resources

article=1433&context=iatul

16 http://www.let.leidenuniv.nl/history/ivh/chap2.htm

17 http://www.techopedia.com/definition/7692/interface-message-processor-imp

18 http://www-03.ibm.com/ibm/history/exhibits/mainframe/mainframe_PR37 0.html

19 http://www.techopedia.com/definition/27856/network-control-protocol-ncp

20 http://www-math.ucdenver.edu/~wcherowi/jcorner/barcodes.html

21 http://www.wired.com/thisdayintech/2010/09/0902first-us-atm/

22 http://www.examiner.com/article/nasdaq-has-opening-day-1971

23 http://www.cs.umd.edu/class/spring2002/cmsc434-0101/MUIseum/applications/firstemail.html

24 http://www.zakon.org/robert/internet/timeline/

25 http://www.cs.utexas.edu/users/chris/think/Cyclades/

26 http://www.thocp.net/timeline/1972.htm

27 http://www.ideafinder.com/history/inventions/internet.htm

28 http://computer.howstuffworks.com/ethernet.htm

Resources

29
http://www.webopedia.com/TERM/L/local_area_network_LAN.ht
ml

30 http://www.pionline.com/article/20131014/PRINT/310149987/
witnesses-to-a-revolution

31 http://www.computerhope.com/jargon/t/telenet.htm

32 http://www.webopedia.com/TERM/I/ISP.html

33 http://www.nsf.gov/about/history/nsf0050/internet/launch.htm

34 http://nrg.cs.ucl.ac.uk/internet-history.html

35 http://highered.mcgraw-
hill.com/sites/dl/free/0073378836/575502/dominick10e_sampl
e_ch11.pdf

36 http://www.historyofcomputercommunications.info/Book/6/6.1
1TCP-TCP-IP76-79%20.html

37 http://www.columbia.edu/~rh120/other/tcpdigest_paper.txt

38 http://www.sff.net/people/jeff.hecht/chron.html

39 http://www.internetsociety.org/internet/what-internet/history-
internet/brief-history-internet

40 http://www.dailymail.co.uk/sciencetech/article-2233035/The-
amazing-adverts-laptop-promise-change-way-work.html

41 http://www.brainstormmag.co.za/index.php?
option=com_content&view=article&id=4378:telecommuting-
timeline

Resources

42 http://ftpguide.com/history.htm

43 http://world-information.org/wio/infostructure/100437611663/1004386594 51

44 http://www.thocp.net/timeline/1982.htm

45 http://www.essortment.com/invented-first-pc-modem-28894.html

46 http://searchsecurity.techtarget.com/definition/IGP

47 http://whatis.techtarget.com/definition/Exterior-Gateway-Protocol-EGP

48 http://www.hkma.gov.hk/media/eng/publication-and-research/reference-materials/banking/ch05.pdf

49 http://www.phil.frb.org/research-and-data/publications/business-review/1985/brmj85jl.pdf

50 http://www.investopedia.com/articles/optioninvestor/10/etf-options-v-index-options.asp

51 http://en.wikipedia.org/wiki/PTAT-1

52 http://www.apple-history.com/

53 http://windows.microsoft.com/en-us/windows/history

54 http://encyclopedia2.thefreedictionary.com/BITNET

55 http://www.cren.net/cren/cren-hist-fut.html

Resources

56 http://www.livinginternet.com/i/ii_eunet.htm

57 http://www.zakon.org/robert/internet/timeline/

58 http://www.internetsociety.org/internet/what-internet/history-internet/brief-history-internet

59 https://www.webfoundation.org/vision/history-of-the-web/

60 http://www.abcteach.com/free/s/science_abacustocomputer.pdf

61 http://www.zakon.org/robert/internet/timeline/

62 http://www.computerhope.com/history/internet.htm

63 http://www.computerhistory.org/timeline/?year=1993

64 http://www.people-press.org/1995/10/16/americans-going-online-explosive-growth-uncertain-destinations/

65 http://brewster.kahle.org/about/

66 http://www.computerhope.com/jargon/v/veronica.htm

67 http://www.salientmarketing.com/seo-resources/search-engine-history/yahoo.html

68 http://www.businessweek.com/1996/09/b34641.htm

69 http://www.internethalloffame.org/internet-history/timeline

70 http://www.greatachievements.org/?id=3706

71 http://dailybarrage.com/2013/10/01/a-brief-history-of-wifi/

Resources

72 http://javascript.about.com/od/reference/p/javascript.htm

73 http://www.google.com/url?
sa=t&rct=j&q=&esrc=s&source=web&cd=5&ved=0CEQQFjA
E&url=http://www.internethalloffame.org/internet-
history/timeline&ei=pHT6Ut2GG4nW0QG8yoHICA&usg=AFQ
jCNFBUMw167zr1J85riLXfGcoFLwDEA&bvm=bv.61190604,d
.dmQ

74 http://en.wikipedia.org/wiki/History_of_Wikipedia

75 http://www.computerworld.com/s/article/69883/Peer_to_Peer
_Network

76 http://oreilly.com/web2/archive/what-is-web-20.html

77 http://www.mediahistory.umn.edu/timeline/2000-2009.html

78 http://www.thocp.net/reference/internet/internet4.htm

79 http://www.theguardian.com/world/1999/nov/09/balkans

80 https://www.eff.org/node/72297

81 https://www.eff.org/nsa-spying/how-it-works

82 https://www.eff.org/nsa-spying/timeline

83 http://money.howstuffworks.com/paypal3.htm

84 http://money.howstuffworks.com/history-e-commerce.htm

85 http://thefinancialbrand.com/25380/yodlee-history-of-internet-
banking/

Resources

86 http://www.ibiblio.org/msmckoy/oclc.html

87 http://www.poynter.org/uncategorized/28693/new-media-timeline-1970/

88 http://www.gutenberg.org/wiki/Gutenberg:The_History_and_P hilosophy_of_Project_Gutenberg_by_Michael_Hart

89 http://www.computerhope.com/history/internet.htm

90 http://inventors.about.com/od/timelines/a/modern_5.htm

91 http://creativecommons.org/about/history

92 http://www.perspectivesonglobalissues.com/0101/OneLaptop. html

93 http://www.theguardian.com/technology/2007/jul/25/media.ne wmedia

94 http://content.time.com/time/magazine/article/0,9171,1990787 ,00.html

95 http://www.geekosystem.com/skype-history-infographic/

96 http://www.socialnomics.net/2013/01/23/the-history-of-twitter/

97 http://www.theage.com.au/articles/2002/11/02/103602709060 5.html

98 http://plaza.ufl.edu/pduffy01/flashmob101/history.html

99 http://wikileaks.org/About.html

100

Resources

http://www.wired.com/threatlevel/2012/03/ff_nsadatacenter/all
/

101 http://www.nytimes.com/2012/02/19/books/review/how-an-egyptian-revolution-began-on-facebook.html?
pagewanted=all&_r=0

102http://america.aljazeera.com/articles/multimedia/timeline-edward-snowden-revelations.html

103
http://www.democracynow.org/2014/2/10/death_by_metadata
_jeremy_scahill_glenn

104 http://en.wikipedia.org/wiki/Cyclic_redundancy_check

105http://en.wikipedia.org/wiki/Multicast

106http://compnetworking.about.com/library/glossary/bldef-kbps.htm

107
http://compnetworking.about.com/cs/wireless80211/g/bldef_wi
fi.htm

108 http://en.wikipedia.org/wiki/File_Allocation_Table

109 http://en.wikipedia.org/wiki/File_Transfer_Protocol

110 http://en.wikipedia.org/wiki/Telnet

111http://wiki.answers.com/Q/What_is_computer_processing_cy
cle

112 http://en.wikipedia.org/wiki/Blind_signature

Resources

113 http://www.google.com/trends/explore%23q=Edward %20Snowden

114 http://www.google.com/trends/explore%23q=Julian %20Assange

115 http://rt.com/usa/snowden-google-search-trends-442/

116 http://www.mirror.co.uk/3am/celebrity-news/miley-cyrus-meet-larry-rudolph-2989569

117 http://www.michelleobrien.net/wp-content/uploads/2013/01/OBRIEN_Assange.pdf

118 http://elitedaily.com/money/the-worlds-10-largest-media-conglomerates/

119 http://privacyink.org/html/MakingSense.pdf

120 http://www.slate.com/blogs/future_tense/2013/08/16/latest_sn owden_documents_prove_proof_of_unlawful_spying_on_am ericans.html

121 http://livepage.apple.com/

122 https://www.aclu.org/blog/national-security/guide-what-we-now-know-about-nsas-dragnet-searches-your-communications

123 https://www.aclu.org/blog/national-security/guide-what-we-now-know-about-nsas-dragnet-searches-your-communications

Resources

124 https://www.aclu.org/blog/national-security/guide-what-we-now-know-about-nsas-dragnet-searches-your-communications

125 https://www.eff.org/nsa-spying

126 https://www.eff.org/nsa-spying/how-it-works

127 http://fromm.robertkeahey.com/wp-content/uploads/2013/07/Session-7-The-Banality-of-'Don't-Be-Evil'-by-Julian-Assange-NYTimes.pdf

128 https://www.eff.org/files/2014/01/02/cryptowarsonepagers-1_final.pdf%23pdfjs.action=download

129 http://siliconangle.com/blog/2013/09/06/bullrun-the-nsa-backdoor-anti-encryption-bug-program-that-breaks-most-encryption-on-the-internet/

130 https://www.eff.org/deeplinks/2013/10/how-nsa-deploys-malware-new-revelations

131 https://www.eff.org/deeplinks/2013/10/how-nsa-deploys-malware-new-revelations

132 http://siliconangle.com/blog/2013/09/06/bullrun-the-nsa-backdoor-anti-encryption-bug-program-that-breaks-most-encryption-on-the-internet/

133 http://www.reuters.com/article/2013/12/20/us-usa-security-rsa-idUSBRE9BJ1C220131220

134 https://www.eff.org/files/2014/01/02/cryptowarsonepagers-1_final.pdf%23pdfjs.action=download

Resources

135 http://www.washingtonpost.com/world/national-security/edward-snowden-after-months-of-nsa-revelations-says-his-missions-accomplished/2013/12/23/49fc36de-6c1c-11e3-a523-fe73f0ff6b8d_story.html

136 https://www.eff.org/nsa-spying/how-it-works

137 http://www.theverge.com/2013/7/17/4517480/nsa-spying-prism-surveillance-cheat-sheet

138 http://www.theverge.com/2013/7/17/4517480/nsa-spying-prism-surveillance-cheat-sheet

139 http://en.wikipedia.org/wiki/Voice_over_IP

140 http://computer.howstuffworks.com/cloud-computing/cloud-storage.htm

141 http://privacyink.org/html/MakingSense.pdf

142 http://privacyink.org/html/MakingSense.pdf

143 https://www.eff.org/deeplinks/2013/08/nsa-spying-three-pillars-government-trust-have-fallen

144 http://fromm.robertkeahey.com/wp-content/uploads/2013/07/Session-7-The-Banality-of-'Don't-Be-Evil'-by-Julian-Assange-NYTimes.pdf

145 http://www.bankinfosecurity.com/alexander-outlines-steps-to-reduce-leaks-a-5843

146 http://www.countercurrents.org/assange091210.htm'

147 http://resistir.info/livros/assange_livro.pdf

Resources

148 https://www.eff.org/deeplinks/2011/02/will-rise-wikileaks-competitors-make

149 http://resistir.info/livros/assange_livro.pdf

150 http://wikileaks.org/

151 http://www.google.com/hostednews/afp/article/ALeqM5geiaM WyifU2kNlin7BdID_aMWtHg

152 https://www.eff.org/deeplinks/2011/11/cablegate-one-year-later-how-wikileaks-has-influenced-foreign-policy-journalism

153 https://www.eff.org/deeplinks/2011/11/cablegate-one-year-later-how-wikileaks-has-influenced-foreign-policy-journalism

154 https://www.eff.org/deeplinks/2011/11/cablegate-one-year-later-how-wikileaks-has-influenced-foreign-policy-journalism

155 http://www.nytimes.com/

156 https://www.eff.org/deeplinks/2013/09/linkedin-commendably-fights-surveillance-transparency-court-multiple-fronts

157 https://www.eff.org/deeplinks/2013/08/nsa-spying-three-pillars-government-trust-have-fallen

158 http://www.washingtonpost.com/world/national-security/nsa-broke-privacy-rules-thousands-of-times-per-year-audit-finds/2013/08/15/3310e554-05ca-11e3-a07f-49ddc7417125_print.html

Resources

159
http://content.time.com/time/world/article/0,8599,2006496,00.
html

160 http://www.theguardian.com/world/2013/jun/09/edward-
snowden-nsa-whistleblower-surveillance?guni=Network
%20front:network-front%20full-width-1%20bento-box:Bento
%20box:Position1

161 http://www.michelleobrien.net/wp-
content/uploads/2013/01/OBRIEN_Assange.pdf

162 http://www.countercurrents.org/assange091210.htm'

163
http://www.theguardian.com/commentisfree/2012/aug/23/wo
men-against-rape-julian-assange

164 https://www.eff.org/deeplinks/2011/11/cablegate-one-year-
later-how-wikileaks-has-influenced-foreign-policy-journalism

165 https://www.eff.org/deeplinks/2011/11/cablegate-one-year-
later-how-wikileaks-has-influenced-foreign-policy-journalism

166 http://www.mediaite.com/tv/glenn-greenwald-denounces-
snowden-smear-campaign-tactic-of-establishment-to-try-to-
demean-people/

167 http://www.topsecretwriters.com/2013/06/the-media-smear-
campaign-against-edward-snowden/

168 http://www.privacysos.org/node/1240

169 http://www.themonthly.com.au/blog/roy-morgan-

Resources

research/2013/06/11/1370907445/new-polling-shows-assanges-wikileaks-leads-new-partie

170 https://www.eff.org/deeplinks/2013/11/how-nsa-mass-surveillance-hurting-us-economy

171 https://www.eff.org/deeplinks/2013/11/how-nsa-mass-surveillance-hurting-us-economy

172 https://www.eff.org/deeplinks/2013/11/how-nsa-mass-surveillance-hurting-us-economy

173 http://voiceofrussia.com/2013_11_28/US-companies-will-lose-35-billion-because-of-Edward-Snowden-9130/

174 http://www.censoring.me/aggregator/sources/2?page=1

175 http://www.theverge.com/2013/7/17/4517480/nsa-spying-prism-surveillance-cheat-sheet

176 http://www.propublica.org/article/nist-to-review-standards-after-cryptographers-cry-foul-over-nsa-meddling

177
http://www.washingtonpost.com/business/technology/microsoft-suspecting-nsa-spying-to-ramp-up-efforts-to-encrypt-its-internet-traffic/2013/11/26/44236b48-56a9-11e3-8304-caf30787c0a9_story.html

178
http://www.washingtonpost.com/business/technology/google-encrypts-data-amid-backlash-against-nsa-spying/2013/09/06/9acc3c20-1722-11e3-a2ec-b47e45e6f8ef_story.html

Resources

179 http://www.washingtonpost.com/blogs/the-switch/wp/2013/11/18/yahoo-is-extending-encryption-across-its-services-but-youll-have-to-turn-it-on-yourself/

180 http://www.wired.com/wiredenterprise/2013/08/mailpile/

181 https://www.eff.org/deeplinks/2011/02/will-rise-wikileaks-competitors-make

182 http://voiceofrussia.com/2013_11_28/US-companies-will-lose-35-billion-because-of-Edward-Snowden-9130/

183 http://www.washingtonpost.com/world/europe/germany-looks-at-keeping-its-internet-e-mail-traffic-inside-its-borders/2013/10/31/981104fe-424f-11e3-a751-f032898f2dbc_story.html

184http://rt.com/news/brazil-nsa-defense-contract-454/

185
http://yhttp:/www.washingtonpost.com/world/europe/germany-looks-at-keeping-its-internet-e-mail-traffic-inside-its-borders/2013/10/31/981104fe-424f-11e3-a751-f032898f2dbc_story.html

186 http://bits.blogs.nytimes.com/2013/11/14/google-employees-speak-out-about-government-spying/?hpw&rref=technology

187 http://www.washingtonpost.com/world/europe/germany-looks-at-keeping-its-internet-e-mail-traffic-inside-its-borders/2013/10/31/981104fe-424f-11e3-a751-f032898f2dbc_story.html

188 http://qz.com/112943/us-firms-worry-edward-snowden-is-

Resources

wrecking-their-business-but-the-patriot-acts-been-doing-that-for-years/

189 http://www.scidev.net/global/digital-divide/news/african-union-set-to-get-tougher-on-cybercrime.html

190 http://www.circleid.com/posts/20121220_wikileaks_of_2012_to_snowden_nsa_leaks_of_2013_internet_governance/

191 http://en.wikipedia.org/wiki/Jane_Austen

192 http://en.wikipedia.org/wiki/Pride_and_Prejudice

193 http://en.wikipedia.org/wiki/Environmental_issues

194 http://en.wikipedia.org/wiki/Royal_prerogative_of_mercy